The Prayer List

The Prayer List

Savanna Watson

Warrior Princess Nation, LLC

Warrior Publishing, a division of Warrior Princess Nation, LLC
6935 Aliante Pkwy Ste 104-423
Las Vegas, NV 89084
for information email info@warriorprincessnation.com

First Print 2025

This book is dedicated to my mom. I call you blessed! Thank you for loving me and letting me use your prayer list to write a whole book, LOL! This one is rightfully yours!

This book served as the training ground and springboard into a journey of bold prayers. Buckle your seatbelts.

Let's Go!

Introduction

This book is, first and foremost, for my mom. My mom and I decided to make a list of areas in our lives in which we needed prayer and spent 30 days praying for each other. I wanted to pray but have something to back up what I was praying. I began looking up different Scriptures from the Bible that talked, mentioned, or related to the requests on her list and began seeing Scriptures applicable to what my mom had written on her prayer list. I started compiling different verses per request, and as I did this, I saw how what we pray for can be answered just by looking at the people who lived out the Scriptures we claim. God answers prayers through His Word, too.

Along this journey of prayer, there were some topics that I am not going to lie were a little intimidating. The intimidation, however, became irrelevant because the Holy Spirit would point me to a specific verse and release the revelation of it and how to claim it in prayer. It was far past the period of prayer my mom and I took for each other, but my notes were sitting there begging for some organization, and they turned into this book. The title of each chapter is the prayer request my mom wrote down, along with the date. My composition book was filled with my notes and what

I encountered through the Scriptures that gave me a foundation to pray from. I hope you enjoy and find some comfort in that all of us have areas where we need prayer. It is okay. Prayer is not just for what we need but for whom we need in our lives every day. There will never be a day when you don't need God. God has got you. I mean, look, you trying to learn about prayer and that you want more of God in your life is an incredible sign. Enjoy this time of reading, and do not worry; we are all going from "glory to glory" (2 Corinthians 3:18 KJV), including the author of this book.

Note from the writer: Do not be too harsh on yourself if you do not get all this right away. I am still learning to this day more and more about each topic. It's going to be okay, and you are doing better than you think you are. Also, as you read each chapter, there are going to be times where I said I was led by the Holy Spirit. I do not mean some big supernatural "led," it was a relational knowing and sense that every single one of us has available to us because of Jesus Christ (John 16:13). My prayer is that Jesus, like in Luke 24:45, would open your minds to understand the Scriptures.

"Then he opened their minds to understand the Scriptures." Luke 24:45

Savanna Watson

*L*ed by the Holy Spirit:

July 22, 2020

"Then Jesus was led by the Spirit into the wilderness to be tempted there by the devil." (Matthew 4:1)

This was the official first day of prayer. I thought of how the Holy Spirit led Jesus after his baptism in the Jordan River. I know in my life when I think of the Holy Spirit leading me, it would be to a magnificent, lush environment where the aroma of everything holy enters my senses, and I lead someone to Christ or give someone a word of knowledge. However, Jesus was led into a straight-up wilderness. Right after he heard God confirm Him as God's Son, in which he is well pleased (Matthew 3:17 KJV), Jesus is led into a wilderness.

I am not saying a wilderness is the only place the Holy Spirit will lead. Nor am I suggesting we are always going to be in hard places, but I am suggesting that a perfect place or idea is not the only place He will lead you.

How comforting is it to know that wherever we are led, God knows the steps we should take and that wherever he leads us, there is provision. There is so much provision to the point of angels tending to you (Matthew 4:11).

The first part of Matthew 4 is Jesus being led into the wilderness and then led to fast. While fasting, the devil came and tempted Jesus. I started from verse 3 and took notes through verse 11. Proverbs 20:12 tells us the Holy Spirit gives us eyes to see and ears to hear. With the promise of this gift, I was able to make some interesting connections in this text that never really stood out before. Let me show you the three attacks of the enemy in this story and perhaps expose the enemy in your own life.

This first attack was after the obvious physical vulnerability and hunger that comes with fasting. *"During that time the devil came and said to him, 'If you are the Son of God, tell these stones to become loaves of bread'" (Matthew 4:3).* The question word in this sentence is, "If." The devil will usually flip the truth. Verse three is a perfect example of this. The devil put the word "if" in front of what Jesus was just told and already knew the truth that was revealed to him and all around him in Matthew 3:17; He is the Son of God. After the devil questioned the truth, he then challenged Jesus to tell the stones to become bread for Jesus to eat (Matthew 4:3). The sin, in this case, would be to turn the stones into bread. To sum up this attack, the enemy questioned Jesus' identity and then added a command to the questioning, setting the trap of sin.

Now to Jesus' response: *"But Jesus told him, "No! The Scriptures say, 'People do not live by bread alone, but by every word that comes from the mouth of God'" (Matthew 4:4).* Now we are going to start with Jesus' response, "No!" This is the answer to the devil's question: even though he commanded something, he first questioned the truth about Jesus. No, was not only no, I am not doing what you say, but also saying no meant that Jesus was saying I know I am the Son of God; I serve God alone.

After answering the question of if, Jesus also answers with the truth from the Scriptures, *"The Scriptures say, 'People do not live by bread alone, but by every word that comes from the mouth of God'" (Matthew 4:4).* Bread can go stale, but the Word of God is always fresh!

In what ways does the enemy question you? Let me rephrase this. What are the questions you have about yourself? Has the enemy answered them for you, or has Jesus? Write out your questions about yourself, and if insecurity starts to rise, take a deep breath. I want you to circle the question word, flip it, and look at what you have left.

Example of flipping the question: Does God really love me? Flip the question word, "Does." Now, write down and read the sentence again.
God really does love me.

Am I enough?
Switch the "Am" and "I" around in this phrase: Am I enough?
I am enough.

Do I matter?
Switch the "Do" and "I" around in this phrase: Do I matter?
I do matter.

This is such a fun exercise that you can do all the time. Now, let us look at the next attack of the enemy.

Attack number two: *"Then the devil took him to the holy city, Jerusalem, to the highest point of the Temple, and said, "If you are the Son of God, jump off! For the Scriptures say 'He will order his angels to protect you. And they will hold you up with their hands, so you won't even hurt your foot on a stone'" (Matthew 4:5-6).*

The devil starts out with the question word "if" yet again. The truth again is revealed by taking what the devil said and flipping it to what God said:

You are the Son of God, (Matthew 3:17). After the question, the devil tells him to jump off the cliff they were on (Matthew 4:6) which would have been a sin.

Now, on to the part where you are probably like, wow, "What about the next part?" is it the truth if the devil said it? The next sentence the devil said is from Psalm 91:11-12. HOWEVER, this is the father of all lies (John 8:44). If you go and read Psalm 91 in its entirety, you can see the devil twisted the truth and took it out of context, similar to the time in the garden.

> *Psalm 91: 9-16 says,*
> *"If you make the LORD your refuge,*
> *If you make the Most High your shelter,*
> *No evil will conquer you;*
> *No plague will come near your home.*
> *For he will order his angels*
> *To protect you wherever you go.*
> *They will hold you up with their*
> *hands*
> *So you won't even hurt your foot on a*
> *stone.*
> *You will trample upon lions and*
> *cobras;*
> *You will crush fierce lions and*
> *serpents under your feet!*
> *The LORD says, "I will rescue those*

who love me.
I will protect those who trust in my name.
When they call on me, I will answer;
I will be with them in trouble.
I will rescue and honor them.
I will reward them with a long life
and give them my salvation."

Notice that out of all the Scriptures, the devil could have used, he managed to find a verse about angels. In verse eleven of Psalm 91, it says, *"For he will order his angels to protect you wherever you go."* I do not think this can be emphasized enough, but the Scripture said, made it a point to not just say "angels" but also to say "his angels." What side is the enemy, this *"angel of light" (2 Corinthians 11:14)* on? NOT God's. This is deception in that, the enemy had the ability to give Jesus what he was offering, but he was trying to make his way and authority (which Jesus came to put back in order) seem more appealing than what God had for Jesus that would be given to all of us today.

Now that we have that covered, look at verse nine of Psalm 91, which says, *"If you make the LORD your refuge, if you make the Most High your shelter."* The "if" in Psalm 91:9 signifies a promise that is conditional. You honor God and make Him your refuge, your shelter; he will honor you with protection, *"angels keeping you from hurting your foot on a stone"* (Psalms 91:12). You see, even though the devil quoted a Scripture, it was out of context.

Jesus' answer: *"Jesus responded, the Scriptures also say, 'You must not test the LORD your God'" (Matthew 4:7)*. Jesus knew the entirety of the promise in Psalm 91, not just a couple of verses. It is not the first nor the last time the devil flipped Scripture around. From the very beginning, the devil has flipped the truth because if he told a point-blank lie to you without being sneaky, you would not believe him.

In the Garden of Eden, both Adam and his wife knew not to eat from the tree of the knowledge of good and evil. Adam's wife recalled this in Genesis 3:3, *"'You must not eat it or touch it; if you do, you will die.'"* Notice that the devil flipped what God said, *"You won't die!" the serpent replied to the woman. "God knows that your eyes will be opened as soon as you eat it, and you will be like God, knowing both good and evil" (Genesis 3:4-5).*

The devil took God's truth, moved some words around, and why it seems so true is because, at first, it was the truth. But the devil took what God meant for good and turned it for evil. But thank God that our God flips the flip of the devil and takes what the enemy meant for evil and turns it for good (Genesis 50:20).

The devil has no authority or truth, so he has to use what God says and flip it. However, taking what I said previously about Psalm 91:11-12, Jesus knew the conditions and the obedience required to those conditions to allow Jesus to receive the promise of God's angels protecting Him. Jesus knew that if He would have jumped, He would have been making the devil his refuge or shelter instead of God, which would be disobedient to the conditions God laid out to receive this promise of safety and protection. Promises are kept because of obedience. Now let us look at the third attack of the enemy and see how the promise in Psalms 91 of his angels protecting you from hurting your foot on a stone manifested.

Third attack: *"Next the devil took him to the peak of a very high mountain and showed him all the kingdoms of the world and their glory. 'I will give it all to you,' he said, 'if you will kneel down and worship me'" (Matthew 4:8-9).* The devil skips the questions this time and instead gives Jesus a choice. If you will kneel down and worship me, is the sin in this attack. You will see why in Jesus' response.

Jesus' response: *"Get out of here, Satan,"* Jesus told him, *"For the Scriptures say, 'You must worship the LORD your God and serve only him'" (Matthew 4:10).* The reason why Jesus did not bow down was because worshiping anyone else but God is a sin (Deut. 6:13). There is no one like our God, so why would we give to anything else that which belongs to God? Maybe Jesus would have had the kingdoms, but he would not be serving God in His Kingdom. Our final truth in this chapter is, that *"the Scriptures say, 'you must worship the LORD your God and serve only him.'"*

In Jesus' final response, He addresses the question that was never stated. Who is this that is tempting me? Jesus took authority and kept relying on the Scriptures.

Now, the whole point of these notes was to talk about being led by the Holy Spirit, and you might be wondering why this seemed more about temptation. I thought this myself, but I remembered why I thought of this story in Matthew when thinking about being led by the Holy Spirit. Go back and look at the verses where Jesus says, "Scripture says…" How do we know what Scriptures to use among all the many possible choices to stand our ground and stay obedient?

Matthew 3:16 says: *"After his baptism, as Jesus came up out of the water, the heavens were opened, and he saw the Spirit of God descending on him like a dove and settling on him."* Did you catch what verse sixteen is throwing down? Jesus received the Holy Spirit. Jesus was led by the Holy

Spirit into the wilderness, where Jesus fasted. Jesus was tempted. But He was still led by the Holy Spirit in not giving into the devil. Here are a few Scriptures about the same Holy Spirit having the right word at the right time. This is the same Holy Spirit that was in Jesus during his time of temptation and life and is now in you (Romans 8:11):

Isaiah 11:2 says, *"And the Spirit of the Lord shall rest upon Him- the Spirit of wisdom and understanding, the Spirit of counsel and might, the Spirit of knowledge and of the reverrential and obedient fear of the Lord-"* (AMPC)

Ezekiel 36:27 says, *"And I will put my Spirit within you and cause you to walk in My statutes, and you shall heed My ordinances and do them."* (AMPC)

There is revelation upon revelation within eight verses, and the same Holy Spirit that led Jesus is leading us. Leading you. It is funny how the stone that the enemy wanted Jesus to turn to bread (Matthew 4:3) did not end up being the stone that Jesus hurt his foot on (Psalm 91:12), and the serpent indeed was and is still crushed (Psalm 91:13). Amen!

Wherever you are in this season, whatever it feels like, the Holy Spirit is with you. The Holy Spirit is your best friend and does not run away when the enemy shows up. The Holy Spirit does not walk out on you when you are going through a dark valley. The Holy Spirit is not afraid of the enemy and the Holy Spirit is not afraid of what the enemy is trying to do. When you made Jesus your Lord and Savior, you were given the Holy Spirit as a gift (John 14:16). Jesus knows this gift well because it is a part of the Father given to Jesus and a part of Jesus given to us (John 17:21).

Being led is not limited to a physical location; it can also mean being led to the right Scriptures. It can mean receiving wisdom to stay in God's promises even when you are literally being tempted. Matthew 4:3-11 is a powerful testimony of how Jesus defeated the enemy by staying in connection with his Father through the Holy Spirit, and we can live like this too.

The Prayer List

Prayer:

Wow! Holy Spirit, thank You for leading us. Thank You for not backing down at the circumstances that are trying to make us back down. Instead, You convict us to rise up and receive our Father's promises (John 16:8). Thank You, Jesus, for being the example and one we can turn to when facing temptation. Thank You that no temptation according to Your Word in 1 Corinthians 10:13 is too much, that You, Father, have created a safe place in Your Word for us to stay in and get rid of the temptation. Thank You that what we ask for is being done now. Holy Spirit, we ask that we could grow even closer with you. Holy Spirit, help me understand You better; help me listen to the guidance You are giving because You heard it from the Father (John 16:13). Thank You that when I do not know what to pray, I can use my heavenly language and trust that You do know what to say (Romans 8:27). Thank You Jesus for being there for me, thank You that You will never leave me or forsake me (Hebrews 13:5). In Jesus' name I pray, AMEN.

And when he comes, he will convict the world of its sin, and of God's righteousness, and of the coming judgment. John 16:8

The temptations in your life are no different from

what others experience. And God is faithful. He will not allow the temptation to be more than you can stand. When you are tempted, he will show you a way out so that you can endure. 1 Corinthians 10:13

When the Spirit of truth comes, he will guide you into all truth. He will not speak on his own but will tell you what he has heard. He will tell you about the future. John 16:13

And the Father who knows all hearts knows what the Spirit is saying, for the Spirit pleads for us believers in harmony with God's own will. Romans 8:27

Don't love money; be satisfied with what you have. For God has said, "I will never fail you. I will never abandon you." Hebrews 13:5

*F*reedom and Victory Over Fear:

July 23, 2020

Who doesn't long for freedom and victory over fear? If someone wrote a book about how to be set free from fear and overcome it, that book would be a best seller in every nation. Wait a minute, a book that tells you how to be free and victorious over fear… Where have I heard about that before? Oh yeah, it is in the Bible! There is verse after verse about how Jesus has set us free from fear and given us victory.

For the Lord is the Spirit, and wherever the Spirit of the Lord is, there is freedom. 2 Corinthians 3:17

So if the Son sets you free, you are truly free. John 8:36

You have given me your shield of victory; your help has made me great. 2 Samuel 22:36

No, despite all these things, overwhelming victory is ours through Christ, who loved us. Romans 8:37

So, if we have freedom and victory, why not over fear? How do I receive this freedom and victory? Ephesians 1:3 says: *"All praise to God, the Father of our Lord Jesus Christ, who has blessed us with every spiritual blessing in the heavenly realms because we are united with Christ."*

Think about that. Not only do we have freedom and victory over fear, but we also have every spiritual blessing in the heavenly realms, and this is only from being united with Christ. When we make Jesus Christ our Lord and Savior, we are united with him. You may look the same and may even feel the same, but you are now a child of God who has been blessed with every spiritual blessing in the heavenly realms.

Now that we know that we are new and are united with Christ, how do we stay in victory? Let us look back at the first Bible verse I put at the beginning of this chapter:

"For the Lord is the Spirit, and wherever the Spirit of the Lord is, there is freedom." 2 Corinthians 3:17

Remind yourself you have the Holy Spirit. Where He is, there is freedom. And since the Holy Spirit is in you, you are free from fear. The fruit of the Spirit is faith, love, joy, peace, patience, kindness, goodness, faithfulness, gentleness, and self-control (Galatians 5:22-23). There is no fear in the fruit of the Holy Spirit.

Exercise: When fear comes in, remind yourself of what the Word of God says. Here are a couple of the abundance of verses that remind you that fear is a liar from the father of all lies:

For God has not given us a spirit of fear and timidity, but of power, love, and self-discipline. 2 Timothy 1:7

But when I am afraid I will put my trust in you. Psalms 56:3

Such love has no fear, because perfect love expels all fear. If we are afraid, it is for fear of punishment, and this shows that we have not fully experienced his perfect love. 1 John 4:18

A great way to stay in God's perfect love is to abide in him. According to Merriam-Webster's Thesaurus, the word abide means "to continue to be in a place for a specific period of time." Abide is a verb, which means it is an action. It is not just something we are; it is what we do. We are the branches, and Jesus is the vine (John 15:5). In my search for more intel on John 15 about vines, I read and learned that a vine provides water and nutrients that allow the branches to produce and yield fruit. So, as a branch, all we are to do is abide. Stay in Jesus. Jesus is the Word of God, so stay in the Word of God.

So the Word became human and made his home among us. He was full of unfailing love and faithfulness. And we have seen his glory, the glory of the Father's one and only Son. John 1:14

This leads me to the next thing I learned about the vinedresser. A farmer takes care of his crops. And the equivalent to a farmer back in Jesus' day was a vinedresser. The vinedresser makes sure there is always a crop, and that old blooms are cut off to be replaced with new ones. The vinedresser is there to make sure the vine and branches are taken care of in every season, with extensive knowledge on how to do so. Since God is the vinedresser, you can bet that He is already there with you. I know that when I first heard of God as a vinedresser, I was a little nervous because I know that vinedressers also prune. When the topic of pruning comes up, especially in Christian circles, most people think of God with a weed whacker ready to chop off branches with a vengeance instead of Him tenderly so as to not damage another part of the branch, taking care of and addressing the needs of the branch.

You do not have to be afraid. In Jesus, there is no fear, just awe, and this reverential respect because his love is perfect. Perfect love casts out fear. You do not have to be afraid that God's grace is going to run out. The last time I checked, a vine does not punish you, and the whole purpose of a vinedresser is to make sure the vine produces healthy fruit as much as possible, not to abuse you or hurt you when you are not doing as well as you should be. In each season, the vinedresser makes sure the branches are prepared for what is to come.

Do not fear! I think one of the main goals of fear, especially as children of God, is to make us doubt the love of the Father for us. If fear can get you to doubt God's love for you, it creates a place of confusion instead of confidence. It not only brings doubt about God but also self-doubt and sends you down the spiral of insecurity. The truth is that God smiles on us because of Jesus. What fear has tried to do to you, God wants to do to fear. God, through faith, wants to make you doubt fear to bring confidence to your heart about many things, including God's love for you and confusion to all the lies of the dark. God wants you to be sure about Him and His love for you. You are God's idea, and He made you fearfully and wonderfully. When you reflect on your maker, those things that were trying to come against you catch a glimpse and reminder of the one who defeated and disarmed them handily.

He canceled the record of the charges against us and took it away by nailing it to the cross. In this way, he disarmed the spiritual rulers and authorities. He shamed them publicly by his victory over them on the cross. Colossians 2:14-15

Woo, let's read this in The Passion Translation: *He cancled out every legal violation we had on our record and the old arrest warrant that stood to indict us. He erased it all- our sins, our stained soul- he deleted it all and they cannot be retrieved! Everything we once were in Adam has been placed onto his cross and nailed permanently there as a public display of cancellation. Then Jesus made a public spectacle of all the powers and principalities of darkness, stripping away from them every weapon and all their spiritual authority and power to accuse us. And by the power of the cross, Jesus led them around as prisoners in a procession of triumph. He was not their prisoner; they were his! Colossians 2:14-15*

Think about that: the thing trying to make you afraid is nothing! It seems big, but it is a liar! It has been disarmed and stripped away of its ability to use its weapon. The only way they get authority is if you give it to them because we receive our authority from Jesus, and He is the only one who can decide to give it to someone. Jesus has given us authority; the only way this is given away is found in the part of this verse of *"...and power to accuse us."* Jesus has set us free, and when we sin, we remember what He did for us, the victory He won on the cross.

This victory is a true victory because **all** our sins were nailed to the cross.

He personally carried our sins in his body on the cross so that we can be dead to sin and live for what is right. By his wounds, you are healed. 1 Peter 2:24

Sin sets you up for death. The sooner you make Jesus your Lord and Savior, the quicker you are getting out of this death trap! When you belong to Jesus, *"...now there is no condemnation for those who belong to Christ Jesus. And because you belong to him, the power of the life-giving Spirit has freed you from the power of sin that leads to death."* Romans 8:1-2

You are free from what Jesus made you free from; this includes fear! You may see fear and be afraid, but you have the mind of Christ (1 Corinthians 2:16), and in Jesus' mind, he remembers how

He stripped that fear of all power and ability to use this power over anyone who has been given authority in Christ! Jesus remembers how he led these principalities around in chains in a parade of Jesus' triumph over them, shaming them with his incredible power and the authority to do so! Go ahead and speak with authority the Word of God!

In every moment, God is looking for someone to show himself strong through (2 Chronicles 16:9). The One who created the heavens and the earth by his Word wants to show Himself strong in you. God made creation out of what He said, not from anything that already existed, but because He spoke them into existence.

By faith we understand that the entire universe was formed at God's command, that what we now see did not come from anything that can be seen. Hebrews 11:3

I believe in every word God spoke. You can give God your weaknesses or areas you struggle with, and God will go to work! I believe there is glory waiting for us to claim a promise straight from the mouth of God. These words are the pathway of all God's promises.

Don't be afraid, for I am with you. Don't be discouraged, for I am your God. I will strengthen you and help you. I will hold you up with my victorious right hand. Isaiah 41:10

Next time you are experiencing fear, remember God spoke light into existence the first day and separated night from day; this created a promise of what He would do the next day because He made the cycle, which would bring a new day.

Then God said, "Let there be light," and there was light. And God saw the light was good. Then he separated the light from the darkness. God called the light "day" and the darkness "night." And evening passed and morning came, marking the first day. Genesis 1:3

We are still living in this promise. Today happened because God made the first day ever. God is faithful to what He created, and that includes you. You mean so much to God. You are precious to God; maybe fear is on your mind, but you have never left God's mind.

You can count on God because He loves to be counted on. When you count on God, it opens up the door of His faithfulness and love, both of which never fail and always endure (Psalm 136:14)! You do not have to know everything; God has not given you that burden. All God asks us to do is believe in him.

Jesus told them, 'This is the only work God wants from you: Believe in the one he has sent.' John 6:29

Fear tries to use the unknown against you; God

uses the unknown for you to give and assure you of an expected end that aligns with His will, which is good, perfect, and pleasing (Romans 12:2). Fear wants to control you leaving you with no choice but one that leads to compromise and death, however, God gives you another choice to follow the way that leads to life.

Today I have given you the choice between life and death, between blessings and curses. Now I call on heaven and earth to witness the choice you make. Oh, that you would choose life, so that you and your descendants might live! Deut. 30:19

Fear robs you of things you have yet to experience: If you are not successful, fear will whisper that success will cause you to fall and end up destroying you. If you are successful, fear will tell you at any moment you are going to fail and lose it all, and then you will be nothing, and no one will want you.

Do you notice how fear never acts alone? One thought creates a spiral that always wants to lead you to destruction. Just as I was writing the ways fear will try to come in, a fearful thought came into my mind and inadvertently tried to keep me from exposing its darkness. Stay humble and armored up so that fear does not have to rob you of the life God has given you to bless you and others. Fear bubbles will come, but bubbles were made to be popped.

Part of staying in victory over fear is also remembering you have victory over everything that tries to separate you from the truth of God and His love for you (Romans 8:38). The truth is that fear is a spirit. Guess what? You know who also is a Spirit? The Holy Spirit! Guess who defeated and conquered fear? Jesus Christ.

But you belong to God, my dear children. You have already won a victory over those people, because the Spirit who lives in you is greater than the spirit who lives in the world. 1 John 4:4

No, despite all these things, overwhelming victory is ours through Christ, who loved us. Romans 8:37

But we are citizens of heaven, where the Lord Jesus Christ lives. And we are eagerly waiting for him to return as our Savior. Philippians 3:20

Oh yeah, that is right, the same power that rose Jesus from the dead lives in you! You are more than a conqueror; you are a citizen of Heaven. Your enemies have been disarmed. Do not let these truths just pump you up; live them. We can talk about how we are free all day, but let us live this truth out loud.

Side note: Maybe you are a new believer in Christ; maybe you have been a believer for decades. Though you have not fully grasped the promise that every spiritual blessing in the heavenly realm now belongs to you (Ephesians 1:3). You keep trying to earn something that can only be received. You keep trying to do it yourself when it is about being united. Freedom and victory over fear have already been taken care of by the divine covenant that we are invited into with the Father, Son, and the Holy Spirit. All we are asked to do is receive this gift, open it, and use it. It is a gift of joy, not strife. Though there are weeds of fear and doubt, they can be pulled so the wheat of God's promises grows taller and closer to their destiny to be used to provide for you and others.

Prayer:

Holy Spirit, thank You that we can receive freedom and victory over anything that tries to harm us, especially fear. Thank You that You have not given us a spirit of fear (2 Timothy 1:7). Thank You for joining us to Jesus and our Father. Thank You, Jesus, for personally carrying my sins in Your body on the cross, and I no longer have to be accused of what You set me free from and forgiven me of (1 Peter 2:24). Thank You, Jesus, for carrying out what the Father planned so that every spiritual blessing in the heavenly realm now belongs to us, who are now united in You (Ephesians 1:3). Thank You, Father, that we are made whole and do not have to run back to what kept us from receiving You, from receiving Your love. Thank You for Your love that casts out fear (1 John 4:18). In Jesus' name, AMEN.

For God has not given us a Spirit of fear and timidity, but of power, love, and self-discipline. 2 Timothy 1:7

He personally carried our sins in his body on the cross so that we can be dead to sin and live for what is right. By his wounds you are healed. 1 Peter 2:24

All praise to God, the Father of our Lord Jesus

Christ, who has blessed us with every spiritual blessings in the heavenly realms because we are united with Christ. Ephesians 1:3

Such love has no fear, because perfect love expels all fear. If we are afraid, it is for fear of punishment, and this shows that we have not fully experienced his perfect love. 1 John 4:18

*F*aith Become Alive:

July 28, 2020

When I saw this on the prayer list, it got me thinking, what is the definition of alive? The "genius" definition I simplified is "not dead." I think the definition of alive we are all looking for when it comes to our faith is full of life or exuberant passion. I mean, faith moves mountains, parts waters, and walks on water. But what about the parts of faith you must have to do what could be seen as little things? Every day, we make decisions and choices, but they may not seem big enough to have faith for. Leaving your faith inactive, and if not used, becomes lifeless.

Jesus says all you need is a little faith to end up moving mountains, even faith the size of a mustard seed (Matthew 17:20). I think the whole point of that picture is seeds were made to grow. However, they do not just shoot up in a day. Plants are not just a one-and-done process.

First, you get a seed. Some seeds you must soak before you bury them in the soil. The soil you have needs to match the needs of the type of plant you desire to grow. Stay with me here. Once the seed is ready to go into the soil, you make about a thumb-deep hole depth, then cover it up with dirt. Now that your seed is in the soil, you tend to it every day. Water it and make sure it is in the proper sunlight. Watch the weather. If you go on vacation, you make sure it still gets taken care of. It seems like the same steps every day. In the midst of the daily choices you make to care for this seed, eventually, it breaks through the soil. Then, the stem and leaves appear. Finally, there is a bloom. Hallelujah, this analogy is almost over.

The bloom is beautiful, and you see the fruit of your labor. The process starts all over again with each seed you plant.

There are times I want the blooms before the leaves when it comes to my faith. I want my faith to be alive, but I want it to be explosive as well. Where is the mountain made for me to overcome? I want the faith to move mountains, but I struggle to spend time reading God's Word. Which is how I get more faith.

So faith comes from hearing, that is, hearing the Good News about Christ. Romans 10:17

To keep my faith alive, I need to first remind myself daily that Jesus is alive. Jesus died AND rose again. Jesus is seated at the right hand of the Father and is praying for me right now. The Holy Spirit is relaying all this to me. Which leads me to this next truth and way of keeping our faith alive.

The Spirit of God, who raised Jesus from the dead, lives in you. And just as God raised Christ Jesus from the dead, he will give life to your mortal bodies by this same Spirit living within you. Romans 8:11

We have been given faith through the Holy Spirit. Our seed of faith is planted in God's faithfulness and is given light and water from Jesus, who is the living water (John 4:10) and the light of the world (John 8:12). We break through the dirt in response to the light and soak up the water to soon produce a leaf or sign of a bloom to come. Then the bloom comes, and we are a display of God's workmanship, God's glory.

Therefore, since we have been made right in God's sight by faith, we have peace with God because of what Jesus Christ our Lord has done for us. Romans 5:1

God keeps this plant going, not us. Once our faith is in bloom, what do we do? What do all blooms of flowers accomplish? They display the beauty of God's growing process, lifting people's spirits. You may be asking what this means. I am not a flower; how do I display God's beauty or lift someone up? It is as if Brother James in the Bible knew we would have this question. If you look at James 2 and start reading from the 14th verse down, the answer to this question and the request my mom wrote down is in the title: *"Faith without Good Deeds is Dead."*

Think about this: faith without you acting on it is dead. We have faith. Some other people who had faith are listed in the eleventh chapter of Hebrews. The stories of these well-known people in the Bible are summed up, and James points out that there came a part in each of these people's stories where they had to act on what they believed to unlock the promises that, to this day, we praise God for. A good example besides the one James mentions of Abraham and Isaac is Noah. God told Noah in Genesis 6 that there was about to be a flood, and Noah needed to build an ark to survive it. It states several times that Noah listened and did as God commanded. Noah heard, believed, and acted. This ark, much like our earlier plant analogy, was a process. This ark was made to carry a pair of each animal, Noah's family, and float on top of the earth. I can only imagine how many people thought Noah was crazy and mocked him as they were going about their day, unaware of what was about to happen.

I feel like there are some days we can relate to Noah. Our ark has already been built, and the flood we are waiting on is God's glory.

For as the waters fill the sea, the earth will be filled with an awareness of the glory of the LORD. Habakkuk 2:14

However, there are people, droughts, and many other circumstances trying to prohibit us from acting on what God says. Phrases like "it is too hard," "you are too small," "there is nothing you can do about it," and "this is just how the world works." Maybe this is how the world works, but we also know how the Word works. We know that our faith matters, and what we do with it matters as well. Sometimes, for our faith to stay alive, we need to build the ark anyway. Every day Noah showed up to work on the ark, or in our case, good deeds we do every day was and is a reminder of what God commanded Noah to do and the promise of safety that would come with it. Every good deed we do is a reminder of the good Jesus has done for us and His promises of blessing and fulfillment that He already accomplished for us.

So, is your faith looking like a plant that has not been watered since last year, and your New Year's resolution was to have a green thumb? You are not alone. If you water a plant according to what it needs and put it in the proper light, it grows.

Just like a plant, if we give our faith the proper water and light, our faith will make it through each season alive and blooming. Jesus offers us living water (John 4:10), and again He is the light of the world (John 8:12). The more time we spend with Jesus, also known as the Word of God, the more we take care of our faith. The way plants grow is used to compare how our faith grows. What plants do as they grow is an analogy for our good deeds. Plants take the carbon dioxide we breathe out into the atmosphere and convert it to oxygen to transmit back into the air. Basically, plants take the bad around them and turn it into something that helps people breathe. Our faith allows us to take what we are given, no matter the circumstances or problems we face, to transform it into something positive that gives life to us and others around us. Maybe some of our faith needs to be revived. If this is where you think your faith is, then all you need to do is ask Holy Spirit to revive you. Go into the Word, read about the "Hall of Faithers" in Hebrews eleven, and let their faith encourage and stir you up. If you are not sure where your faith is, ask Holy Spirit and listen. Faith is not something you buy yourself; it is a gift you receive and use (1 Corinthians 12:9). You need some faith? Here is a simple way to start to activate it. The declaration I want to give you comes from Hebrews 6:12.

Then you will not become spiritually dull and indifferent. Instead, you will follow the example of those who are going to inherit God's promises because of their faith and endurance.

This Scripture is a seed of faith. I want you to read it back to yourself aloud. Then act on it and declare the following below over yourself:

- **I will not become spiritually dull and indifferent.**
- **I show the love God has shown me to others every day.**
- **I am following the examples of those who are going to inherit God's promises because of their faith and endurance.**

Every day we have choices to make and no matter how small they seem; God has given us "faith to bring our hopes into reality and set a foundation to acquire the things we long for." Hebrews 11:1 (TPT)

Prayer:

Father, thank You for faith. Thank You for what You said in Hebrews 11:1, *"NOW FAITH is the assurance (the confirmation, the title deed) of the things [we] hope for, being the proof of things [we] do not see and the conviction of their reality [faith perceiving as real fact what is not revealed to the senses]" (AMPC).* Wow, thank You for the incredibly kind gift of faith! You knew, Father, that there were going to be times when it felt like You were not with us; we could not see You like we had before. BUT because of faith, we can be assured You are with us. Your promises are with us. We are spiritually alive now because it is no longer the spirit of the world that lives in us; it is the Spirit of the Word of God (Romans 8:9). Holy Spirit is the one who makes us spiritually alive. Holy Spirit, revive my faith. I ask for the gift of faith. Thank You for reminding me that I am no longer dead spiritually. Thank You, Father, for life abundantly. In Jesus' name, AMEN.

"NOW FAITH is the assurance (the confirmation, the title deed) of the things [we] hope for, being the proof of things [we] do not see and the conviction of their reality [faith perceiving as real fact what is not revealed to the senses]. Hebrews 11:1 AMPC

But you are not controlled by your sinful nature. You are controlled by the Spirit if you have the Spirit of God living in you. (And remember that those who do not have the Spirit of Christ living in them do not belong to him at all.) Romans 8:9

*T*rust Wholeheartedly:

July 28, 2020

      Trust wholeheartedly; this is something so many Christians want, but there seems to be a barrier. What is this barrier, though? The Scriptures say the veil or barrier from fully receiving God and, in turn, trusting Him has been ripped and is no longer an obstacle (Matthew 27:51). God has already put in everything it would take to trust Him, with promises, sacrifice, protection, and His Word. Where are these obstacles coming from? What are these obstacles? How do I get rid of them? Once I get rid of the obstacles, what is trust?

      The biggest obstacle that none of us can remove is sin. Only Jesus can take away sin and make a way to the Father.

> *Everyone who sins is breaking God's law, for all sin is contrary to the law of God. And you know that Jesus came to take away our sins, and there is*

no sin in him. Anyone who continues to live in him will not sin. But anyone who keeps on sinning does not know him or understand who he is. 1 John 3:4-6

Once you get this obstacle out of the way, sometimes the enemy will start adding them, and what is even crazier is he will use you to do it. Ahhh! What?! When I say the enemy can use you to put up obstacles, I do not mean he possesses you. What I do mean is that we are a new creation; the old us is dead to sin, buried, and the child of God has risen. Being a new creation, we have been given authority.

This means that anyone who belongs to Christ has become a new person. The old life is gone; a new life has begun! 2 Corinthians 5:17

Look, I have given you authority over all the power of the enemy, and you can walk among snakes and scorpions and crush them. Nothing will injure you. Luke 10:19

This authority is ours to use through Christ, and it will be used one way or another. What the enemy does is try and bring up the old you. Old thoughts, habits, memories, and relationships take away the authority God has given you to be free from the old with the intent to accuse you of what Jesus has actually freed and forgiven you of.

You are probably wondering, Savanna, what does authority or any of this have to do with trusting God wholeheartedly? The reason why I bring authority up is because we need to stand on the foundation of the Word, from which our authority comes, and not the shakiness of our knowledge and understanding.

You need to use the authority found in the Word of God through Jesus Christ to help you clear out what is keeping your heart from truly trusting God. Here is an example of how you can use the Word to trust God wholeheartedly. The Bible verse we will be using as a building block to building trust is Proverbs 3:5, which says: "Trust in the LORD with all your heart; do not depend on your own understanding."

A side note of encouragement: Trusting the Lord wholeheartedly is a command, and the fact that you want to follow this command is a great sign. A lot of times, our hearts are in the right direction, but there are obstacles from our past we bring up because we have not changed how we practice running our race.

Philippians 3:14 tells us that we are all called to run the race of life with God. Before any race, you practice, but when you receive Jesus into your heart, you run on a different racetrack than the world's racetrack that you were previously on. You cannot keep practicing on the world's racetrack when you are now on the Word's racetrack. That would be extra work you do not have to do and wear you down quicker.

Now that you have entered into the new race let's take down the obstacles of the previous course you were on and look at the new things that will give you endurance. The best way to start this off is with the Word.

- *Never forget the things I have taught you. Store my commands in your heart. Proverbs 3:1*
- *Never let loyalty and kindness leave you! Tie them around your neck as a reminder. Write them deep within your heart. Proverbs 3:3*
- *Seek his will in all you do, and he will show you which path to take. Proverbs 3:6*

The next step is to know what the definition of trust is. Trust, according to Merriam-Webster's Dictionary definition, is "the sure reliance on the character, ability, strength, or truth of someone or something." So, if doubt is the opposite of trust, then doubt means "you are not sure of how you can rely on someone's character ability, strength, or truth of that person."

Taking what we have just read, let us make a formula for trust. The first proverb we started out with was the fifth verse of Proverbs three, which stated, *"Do not depend on your own understanding."* This is the first part of our formula:

Do not depend on your own understanding.

Next, we will take verse one of Proverbs three, which is, *"Never forget the things I have taught you. Store my commands in your heart."* This is the second part of the formula:

Never forget the things I have taught you. Store my commands in your heart.

When you add, *"Do not depend on your own understanding"* + *"Never forget the things I have taught you. Store my commands in your heart,"* you get a sum of trust. The old formula we need to get rid of is depending on our own understanding + relying on the world + the opinions of other people. The Word's formula is tested and has been used in good times and bad. However, the world's formula for trust only works when everything is perfect, and even then, it is risky.

Another great thing about the Word's formula for trust is as you read the Scriptures, you can start adding new revelation to it, so it becomes a guide throughout your whole life. To trust God wholeheartedly in the race you are now running is going to require you to lay down the old way of doing things and pick up the authority that has been given to you to receive the new things. It will help so much if you let go of what you thought things should look like and start learning how

God actually sees them. Get rid of everything the world told you about God and learn who the Word describes God as for yourself. The only way to see the Father is by seeing Jesus.

Jesus replied, 'Have I been with you all this time, Philip, and yet you still don't know who I am? Anyone who has seen me has seen the Father! So why are you asking me to show him to you?' John 14:9

As you seek Jesus in the Word, you will begin to read about God's character, and you can trust the one who created the foundation of trust. A great way to ease into trusting God is by reading the names of God. These names are who He was, is, and always will be because *"God is the same yesterday, today, and forevermore" Hebrews 13:8.* The provision, season, times, relationships, and world might change, but in James 1:17 it says, *"He will never cast a shifting shadow."*

Side note of encouragement: This is going to take time, so don't be too hard on yourself if you have a hard time with trust at first. God has given us time; give yourself some time as well. The first step always seems like the hardest and scariest, but even a tiptoe toward God will launch you into a whole new direction that leads to abundant life. Try it; Holy Spirit is right there as your best friend.

The Holy Spirit is not going to laugh at your

baby steps, though there is joy in them. I know that in my own life, I trusted God but was not always so sure about trusting who He created me to be. I can write, but can I really write a book? I can paint, but could I really be successful in that? I see what the world sees and do not focus on how the Word sees me. I will spend more time on the prayer request of trusting yourself in the next chapter and the chapter of *"Love My Body and Self Esteem"* to give more guidance in this area where we are learning throughout our lives.

Prayer:

Father, thank You for Your trust. Thank You that we can trust You. There is nothing in You that should keep us from trusting You (1 John 1:5). Thank You for cleansing my heart of all the hurt, pain, brokenness, and circumstances of my past today (Psalms 51:10). I am not denying what happened to me, but instead choosing to trust in the one who turns what the enemy meant for evil into good (Genesis 50:20). Thank You; now I am free to trust You with my whole heart. Thank You that You know how to put my heart back together (Psalm 147:3). You know where each piece goes and how to make it stronger. Father, I put my whole trust, my spirit, mind, will, and emotions in You (Matthew 22:37). You are trust, and I believe You will never ever fail me (Deut. 31:6). In Jesus' name, AMEN.

This the message we heard from Jesus and now declare to you: God is light, and there is no darkness in him at all. 1 John 1:5

Create in me a clean heart, O God. Renew a loyal spirit within me. Psalms 51:10
You intended to harm me, but God intended it all for good. Genesis 50:20

He heals the brokenhearted and bandages their

wounds. Psalm 147:3

Jesus replied, 'You must love the LORD your God with all your heart, all your soul, and all your mind.' Matthew 22:37

So be strong and courageous! Do not be afraid and do not panic before them. For the LORD your God will personally go ahead of you. He will neither fail you nor abandon you. Deuteronomy 31:6

Savanna Watson

*L*ove Myself:

July 28, 2020

A common theme in the prayers my mom gave me is that these are probably all prayers on our lists. Loving who you are seems easy, but it can be hard when you see yourself as what you have done, your mistakes, your problems, your insecurities, and anything else that would give you a reason not to love yourself. I have great news for you, though; you do not have to rely on your own victory or success for a reason to love who you are! You can receive the love that came out of Jesus' obedience and love for the Father! And this was all because God, Jesus, and the Holy Spirit love you. Yes, you! You are who God says you are now. Therefore, you are loved by God right now!

That is what the Scriptures mean when God told him, "I have made you the father of many nations." This happened because Abraham believed in the God who brings the dead back to life and who creates new things out of nothing. Romans 4:17

How does God define love?
According to 1 Corinthians 13:4-7 Love is:
- » Patient and kind
- » Not jealous or boastful or proud
- » Not rude
- » Not demanding of its own way
- » Not irritable
- » Not keeping a record of being wronged
- » Not rejoicing about injustice
- » Rejoicing when the truth wins out
- » Never giving up
- » Never losing faith
- » Always hopeful
- » Able to endure through every circumstance

This is the kind of love God loves us with and the kind of love we should love Him, others, and ourselves with as well. The key to loving yourself is in the request itself. Loving yourself requires you to love yourself the way God has defined love. Yeah, that is right, you can love yourself! You do not have to take on this idea that you are called to love others and avoid yourself. In Mark 12:31, he says to *"love your neighbor as yourself."* We are called to love others, but this verse also points out to love yourself. How can you give love to others that you do not even give to yourself? Maybe you are trying your best to love others, but it is hard. You might argue, well, no one has ever loved me, so I have an excuse not to love. Actually, you do have someone who loves you, even if the whole world hates you, and it is God who loves you!

For this is how God loved the world: He gave his one and only Son, so that everyone who believes in him will not perish but have eternal life. John 3:16

Love tends to hang in the balance of being the easiest thing at times and the hardest. I also recognize that everybody's relationships and experiences with love are going to be different. BUT the way it could be a little easier is by loving yourself and others God's way.

You have a reason to love. Put it this way: say you need to give someone a sandwich, and you say I will give you a sandwich, but you do not have a sandwich. You must have what you give; otherwise, you will be giving nothing. You want to love yourself; accept the gift of love that God is for you. This way, you will have what you are called to give.

I know this may make your toes curl because, as Christians, we are called to be humble and selfless (which we are). But, so many times, when the world says to love yourself, it is not God's definition of love (which is humble and selfless). As Christians, we have the right command of how to love others and love ourselves in a way that brings glory to God. God loves you. The more you learn about how God created you and why and how He loves you, it will allow you to love yourself and others the way He always intended.

Maybe your toes did not curl when I said love yourself; maybe what makes you question this is that you do not like who you are or how you look. Perhaps you do not even look in a mirror and try to avoid them because all you will see are mistakes, wrinkles, fat, acne, people's opinions, and so many other things insecurity brings up so that it can open the door to fear. Then fear brings doubt, and soon, a glance in the mirror turns into a horror movie soundtrack only you can hear. Let me tell you, first off, there is hope! God has given us a new song and soundtrack to our lives, and it is beautiful (Psalm 40:3).

There is hope because I have been there. In art, we had to do self-portraits, and we had to look into a mirror; I dreaded it because I knew I would see all the mistakes and flaws that I purposely avoided by not looking into a mirror or having my picture taken. I was a Christian then, but knowing what I know now about how the enemy comes in and questions the truth, I see that those were lies. Did I have acne and some baby fat? Yes. Did I want to get rid of them? Yes! However, when I am scared to look in the mirror or at a picture, I remind myself of how God, my creator, sees me. I remember that my acne and flaws did not make Jesus even flinch when He chose to die on the cross for me so that I may enjoy how He created me.

I am the living one. I died, but look- I am alive forever ever! And I hold the keys of death and the grave. Rev. 1:18

He isn't here! He is risen from the dead, just as he said would happen. Come, see where his body was lying. Matthew 28:6
The thief's purpose is to steal and kill and destroy. My purpose is to give them a rich and satisfying life. John 10:10

Some of those memories feel like scars now, but Jesus knows about scars. Scripture says that Jesus took so many beatings on the day He died for you and me. People did not even recognize that he was a human because of everything that was done to him.

But many were amazed when they saw him. His face was so disfigured he seemed hardly human, and from his appearance, one would scarcely know he was a man. Isaiah 52:14

Jesus loves the way you look; he saw that face knitted together by the Father in your mother's womb (Psalm 139:15). He recognizes the freckles you have from the day the Father painted them there one by one. And your skin color is mixed with originality and heaven's hues just for you. Zephaniah 3:17 says, *"For the LORD your God is living among you. He is mighty savior. He will take delight in you with gladness. With his love, he will calm all your fears. He will rejoice over you with joyful songs."*

This can be hard to believe; believe it anyway. Do not wait for your feelings to catch up to feel this; it is a gift from God for you right now, wherever you are or how you look. When you let the light in, the darkness must flee. Every lie must bow on its knees and come under the obedience of Jesus Christ! This is not just a fact; it is the truth. It is the Word of God that says you are a masterpiece (Ephesians 2:10), and unlike people's opinions and comments often made without thinking, the Word has been tested several times (Psalm 12:6) so you can take each promise to heart and taste and see just how good God is.

I cannot tell how you feel after this chapter, but I know that this makes me pumped and equipped to see that I am beautiful, I am better than beautiful, and I am a piece of the Master himself. You are, too. You did not earn this, but instead, you get to freely receive it! Take it; do not believe lies that set you up to keep you chained to the past or people's opinions that keep you from the life and future God wants you to have right now.

And we have received God's Spirit (not the world's spirit), so we can know the wonderful things God has freely given us. 1 Corinthians 2:12

Love yourself! The following page has some ways to practice this every day.

Ways to love yourself every day God's way:

1. Be patient and kind to your body, heart, mind, and soul.
2. When you mess up, forgive yourself and get back up again.
3. Don't be mad when someone has something you want; celebrate the promises you have in Christ.
4. When you are excelling (and you will), be confident and humble, knowing where your victory comes from.
5. Do not demand your own way, but receive and be open to what the Word of God can open you up to.
6. Never give up on yourself; God hasn't.
7. Celebrate the truth.

8. Ask for faith.
9. Keep on hoping!
10. Keep going with the strength you have, and give God your weaknesses.

Prayer:

Father, thank You for loving me. I receive Your love for me right now. Thank You for showing me how to love myself and love others. Thank You that Your love is not a selfish love but one that knows others' values as well as our own. Thank You, Holy Spirit, for giving us the ability to receive God's love. Thank You that the hope You have given us, Father, *"...will not lead to disappointment. For we know how dearly God loves us, because he has given us the Holy Spirit to fill our hearts with his love." (Romans 5:5)* Thank You, Jesus, for demonstrating what love is (1 John 4:19). Thank You for Your love for us. In Jesus' name, we love You too, AMEN.

And this hope will not lead to disappointment. For we know how dearly God loves us, because he has given us the Holy Spirit to fill our hearts with his love. Romans 5:5

We love each other because he loved us first. 1 John 4:19

*B*e Content:

July 28, 2020

    The introduction I am going to make for this chapter is the following statement:
"The more you rely or trust in things such as 'perfect' circumstances, money, life, friends, relationships, family, clothes, houses, cars, and the very presence of things in your life, the less content you will be."
I want to make it clear God does and will continue to prosper us! This trust in things is not to say God does not bless us with things, but it is saying we worship God and not the things. We do not put our trust in things; we put our trust in God.

    I want you to read aloud Psalm 23, or if you are in a coffee shop or area where this would be a little weird, just whisper. As you read it, I want you to take the words "my, I, and me" in the Psalm and replace them with your name.

The Lord is _____ shepherd;
_____ shall not want.
He makes _____ to lie down
In green pastures;
He leads _____ beside the still waters.
He restores _____ soul;
He leads _____ in the paths of
Righteousness
For His name's sake.
Yea, though _____walks through
The valley of the shadow of death,
_____ will fear no evil;
For you are with _____;
Your rod and your staff,
They comfort _____.
You prepare a table before _____ in
The presence of _____ enemies;
You anoint _____ head with oil;
_____ cup runs over.
Surely goodness and mercy
Shall follow _____
All the days of _____ life;
And _____ will dwell in the House
Of the Lord forever. Psalm 23 NKJV

Woo, that may have felt weird, but that is what God is speaking over you, and it is to remind you the Word of God can be as close to you as you let it. There are promises of God eager, with great anticipation, waiting for someone to claim them. There are certain promises, like Psalm 23, that are usually read when we have tried everything to be happy or fulfilled and are worn out from the work that it takes. It is a lot of work to be happy in our own strength, let alone be joyful.

Psalm 23 is about God taking care of us, not us taking care of ourselves. Things did not bring the peace David was longing for. Instead, it was God leading him. God is our provider, but he is also our guide. I know for me; I want God to bring me everything. Actually, I want you to bring me everything and throw God in the mix. I want to bring myself, save myself, I, I, I, ayayay, but there will come a point in your journey with your Savior; you will realize it is He. It is Jesus who leads; you follow. Even when it looks like you are leading, it is a result of you following and serving Him first. It is Jesus who provides; you receive. Much like our exercise, Jesus already spoke the Word; the only burden you have is to insert your name into each one as a covenant heir of God and live them out. They are yours, not the devils!

He sent out his word and healed them, snatching them from the door of death. Psalms 107:20

Suddenly, the meaning of content, referring to the quantity or how much we have, turns into what we are really searching for, which is content in terms of quality. Be led by the Father. When we follow where the Father is taking us, we discover what we are really searching for. A lot of times, we get so caught up in all the details about the destination to which God is bringing us, but along the journey, the need for details seems to drift away as you gaze more and more into the eyes of your guide, God. Suddenly, the only destination you are concerned with is how to reach His heart because no matter where you are or where you are going, you have found God's heart is your life, joy, peace, and everything you have been looking for your whole entire life.

The whole point of Psalm 23 is not about what we get but who we get to receive it from and with. God is as much a part of what you receive as you are. Enjoy God because when the wells of the world dry up, God will still be there. When seeking everything, you will learn who your everything actually is.

John 4:4-26 sums it up perfectly by declaring, *You do not need to keep looking for other wells to satisfy you when the well of life, Jesus, is right in front of you. He is the only one who truly knows you. Give him your cup to fill.* **(prophetic emphasis added to personalize Scripture)**.

Jesus is not going to disappoint like all those

other wells. There are so many relationships, jobs, and people that looked and were advertised as promising but left you more hurt. Jesus is not a buy-in one-time deal that leaves you worse off than you were before. Jesus is a life guarantee that whether it is good or bad, He is going to work on your behalf.

And we know that God causes everything to work together for the good of those who love God and are called according to his purpose for them. Romans 8:28

In fact, right now, He is in Heaven telling the Father about you- good things, for He is our Advocate (Romans 8:34). Jesus is praying for you and has given you the Holy Spirit to be your best friend and guide so that you will never run out of what you need to have an abundant life.

Jesus loves you so much. Please, I can hear Jesus saying, I AM the well that was sent to satisfy you. Jesus knows your heart and all the pain; He knows where to add and upgrade. Jesus only does what He sees the Father doing. The Father loves you! In fact, He loves you too much to see you settle. You are on a firm foundation that does not settle. If your foundation does not settle, neither should you. You are called and anointed. You are meant to be filled by the One who created you. Please, do not settle for

anything less.

He lifted me out of the pit of despair, out of the mud and the mire. He set my feet on solid ground and steadied me as I walked along. Psalms 40:2

Prayer:

Be it unto me, Father (Luke 1:38, KJV). The words I just read of You be the bread of life in my life, be it unto me. Woe is me! I am undone (Isaiah 6:5, KJV). Thank You for being my Shepherd and leading me to You (John 10:14). Keep me close. Though I may come in broken and fall apart, I grow on a foundation that never will be broken or fall apart. The secret is in the foundation of my freedom and salvation, my Savior, Jesus Christ. I receive Father, be it unto me. In Jesus' name, AMEN.

And Mary said, Behold, I am the servant of the Lord; may it be done unto me according to thy word. And the angel departed from her. Luke 1:38 KJV

Then I said, Woe is me! For I am undone. Isaiah 6:5 KJV

"I am the good shepherd; I know my own sheep, and they know me…" John 10:14

*L*ove My Body and Self-Esteem:

July 29, 2020

I combined love, my body, and my self-esteem because one tends to affect the other. When you have high self-esteem, you are more likely to love your body, but when you have low self-esteem, it is easier not to love your body. These are temporary bodies, but they are bodies that God has given us. Like any other gift, we can lose interest if we are not putting in time and care into what we have received. Other times, we can overuse a gift. In both instances, we can find ourselves wishing we had new gifts or someone else's gift, but what you have is special and is made to bring the Father glory. We are going to dive into how to love your gift, aka your body.

In the opening, I used the analogy of receiving a gift to emphasize that God has given us a body. Our body changes and matures to the point where science would say there are processes we can expect at certain times in our lives for our body to complete and other times where it cannot. Well, science, let me introduce you to Sarah. Sarah sticks out to me so much when talking about loving our bodies since her miracle took place in the womb of her body.

Sarah never had a son. She even mentioned how she could not even have a son when her body was fit to do it (Genesis 16:2). Now fast-forward to ninety years of age, and God was expecting Sarah to expect a miracle that would take place in her body. If you are laughing at Sarah's situation, you are not the only one; Sarah laughed too (Genesis 18:12). See, even before Sarah heard the angels that came to Abraham to say Sarah would have a son, she tried giving Abraham a son a different way. Sarah knew she could not have a child in her own strength and stated, *"The LORD has prevented me from bearing children,"* and Sarah's idea was to give Abraham her servant, Hagar, as a wife, and they have a child together. Sarah's idea backfired (Genesis 16:2). Sarah got the opposite of a blessing.

Sarah's idea. What is your idea of how to bring to pass the promises of God into your life?

What plan do you have? Is this plan based around what disqualifies you? That is what a lot of our plans are when it comes to believing God for a miracle or answer to prayer. Do you want to know God's plans for you? How he plans for you?

God plans his promises according to and around what does qualify you, his Son. In order to get this, though, you will have to bring your sins and weaknesses, but this is not the end of the plan God has for you; it is only the beginning. You see what you are not, but then see what God has seen inside of you this whole entire time. Sarah saw herself as a wife; God saw her as a mother. Abraham saw himself as a husband; God saw him as a father. You cannot have a father without a mother. Isn't this so in our relationship with Jesus? Without the Father sending his Holy Spirit in Mary (Luke 1:35), we would not have our deliverer. Without the Father sending Jesus and Jesus sending the Holy Spirit, we would not have deliverance and freedom of sin to step into the destiny God planned for us long ago.

Sarah got so caught up in the how of the promise, forgetting the who of the covenant. Sarah's plan was to alter her covenant with Abraham so she could see the promise but not experience it. Do not alter your covenant with God so that you can see the promise your way but not experience the promise God's way. Do not take your name out of the Covenant of Blood you have with Jesus, and do not try to add the ways of the world into it just because they do not match your timeline.

Sarah got caught up in what she could think, feel, and see. Sarah thought that her body was old; she felt that her body was old, and she saw that she was too old. God was expecting Sarah to believe in His ability and faithfulness to come through on what He promised her, not her body's ability to come through for her. How do you see your body? What parts steal the faith God has given you to be able to bring Him glory? When you start focusing on the imperfections in your life, you will lose focus on who you truly are.

Sarah got so caught up in what her body could not do anymore that she tried to take herself out of one of the biggest blessings God would give her. Yes, the promise was about the son, nations, and blessings of Abraham we still receive to this day. The promise was also for Sarah. God wanted to bless Sarah, too. God wants to bless you, too, at whatever stage your body is in. It is not the body that needs to do the impossible; that is God's job through your body. It is only your job to believe.

Jesus answered them, "This is the work of God, that you believe in him who he has sent." John 6:29 ESV

You are housing the Holy Spirit on the inside of you. Let him move you and show you how the Father truly sees you.

Self-Esteem. When you say you want high self-esteem, what do you mean?

The definition of self-esteem, according to the Oxford Dictionary, is "confidence in one's own worth or abilities; self-respect." Self-esteem levels that are based on the Word of God should be the aim since we know our own worth and abilities come from God. We are confident because God is our confidence. We are made in God's image and are His children, so we know the source of where our worth and abilities come from.

But blessed are those who trust in the LORD and have made the LORD their hope and confidence. Jeremiah 17:7

So God created human beings in his own image. In the image of God he created them; male and female he created them. Genesis 1:27

So you have not received a spirit that makes you fearful slaves. Instead, you received God's Spirit when he adopted you as his own children. Now we call him "Abba, Father." Romans 8:15

There I will go to the altar of God, to God- the

source of all my joy. I will praise you with my harp, O God, my God! Psalms 43:4

The self-esteem people want higher is usually based on their own worth and abilities that they do not think come from God but from themselves. This belief sets you up for a long roller coaster of a journey to try and have high self-esteem since you do not have a source of identity to lean into when your worth and abilities are challenged.

Using Sarah as our example again, this time for self-esteem, notice that before she received the promise in her body, she received it in her identity. In Genesis 17:15 it says that God told Abraham Sarai's name would no longer be Sarai; it would be Sarah. I was looking for the definition of both Sarai and Sarah and found what I was not looking for. What I mean is I just typed in *"Sarai name definition,"* and the first thing that popped up was an explanation that described the journey of a name. What stuck out to me was that they basically broke it down, saying that Sarai was the name Abraham's wife had from where they had previously been. The wife that could not have children even when her body was at an expecting age, the wife that came along with Abraham when he was Abram, leaving everything they knew behind. The next thing you know, Sarai is no longer Sarai but Sarah.

Then God said to Abraham, "Regarding Sarai,

your wife- her name will no longer by Sarai. From now on her name will be Sarah." Genesis 17:15

It was one letter that changed in her name, but she was no longer where she came from or what they called her; she was who God called her to be.

What does this have to do with you and your self-esteem? I think the story of Abraham and Sarah is a lot like ours. We start out with one identity as we are born a slave to sin, but then Jesus comes in, and before we receive every promise in the heavens, our name changes. There is no more shame on our name, no more death, only grace, and redemption. We are now in Christ, and though we may look or feel the same, our name has changed. Our name now has redemption on it. It seems like a small change, but it is the greatest change of all, greater than what anybody could see with their natural eyes.

The nations will see your righteousness. World leaders will be blinded by your glory. And you will be given a new name by the LORD's own mouth. Isaiah 62:2

From guilt to grace, doubt to faith, worry to worship, hate to love, all because our name is now registered in Heaven above (Luke 10:20). You, too, are now known for who you put your trust in, not what happened to you. Your faith is what sets you apart. You are complete in Christ. You are known by where you are going, not where you have been. Remember that self-esteem can be defined as confidence. To be confident in the Lord takes you to another level of high self-esteem. You learn that you are highly esteemed in the Lord's eyes (Daniel 10:11, NIV).

» **You are set apart**
(Deut. 14:2)

» **You are chosen**
(Romans 8:29)

» **You are made in God's image**
(Genesis 1:27)

» **You are victorious**
(1 John 5:4)

» **You are more than a conqueror**
(Romans 8:37, ESV)

» **You are an overcomer**
(John 16:33)

» **You are favored**
(Song of Songs 6:9, TPT)

- » You are highly favored
  (Luke 1:28, KJV)

- » You are anointed
  (Psalms 92:10)

- » You are a child of the Most High God
  (Psalms 82:6)

- » You are loved
  (Song of Songs 2:10, TPT)

- » You are saved
  (Romans 10:10)

- » You are forgiven
  (Colossians 1:14)

- » You are blessed
  (Deut. 28:6)

- » You are filled with the fruit of God's very
  own Spirit
  (Galatians 5:22-23)

- » You are an heir to the throne
  (Romans 8:17, KJV)

» You are the bride of Christ
(Revelation 21:2)

» You are a believer
(Acts of the Apostles 19:18)

» You are a gift from above
(James 1:17)

» You are a miracle
(Psalms 139:14)

» You are more than your past
(Isaiah 43:18 AMP)

» You are more than what people label you as
(1 Peter 2:9)

» You are called higher than what people
could make room for you to be in their eyes
(1 Samuel 16:7)

» You are a prayer warrior
(1 Thessalonians 5:17)

» You are strong
(Ephesians 6:10)

» You are able to crush serpents and
  scorpions under your feet
  (Luke 10:19)

» You are united with Christ
  (Ephesians 1:3)

» You are seated in heavenly places
  (Ephesians 2:6)

» You are a foreigner in a distant land
  (Hebrews 13:14, TPT)

» You are here for a purpose
  (Romans 8:28, TPT)

» You are in the palm of God's hand
  (Isaiah 62:3)

» You are covered in his feathers
  (Psalm 91:4)

» You are brave
  (Psalm 27:14)

» You are courageous
  (Psalms 31:24)

» You are Spirit-filled
(Acts of the Apostles, 13:52)

» You are a new creation
(2 Corinthians 5:17)

» You are reborn
(John 1:13)

» You are going places
(Acts of the Apostles 9:32)

» You are going to achieve greater things
than what has been the standard in your
family
(2 Corinthians 5:15, MSG)

» You are beautiful
(Song of Songs 1:15, TPT)

» You are accepted
(John 6:37)

» You are enough
(Ephesians 2:8)

» You are you
(Psalms 139:16)

» God loves you right now
(John 16:27)

» You are precious to God right now
(Daniel 10:11).

Savanna Watson

Prayer:

Wow! Thank You, Father, for revealing my identity to me. Thank You that I am anointed (Psalms 92:10). Thank You for blessing me. Thank You for my body. I ask for a specific way I can take care of my body right now. I ask You for and receive the healing of my body, inside and out, that is mine because, by Jesus Christ's stripes, I am healed (Isaiah 53:5, KJV). You are my healer. Father, I receive healing in my thoughts, and that every insecurity is now replaced with confidence in who You say I am. Because who You say I am and what You say about me is true, for You do not lie (Numbers 23:19, ESV). Thank You, Father, that I am highly esteemed (Daniel 10:11 NIV). Thank You that the thoughts You have about me are precious and outnumber the grains of sand (Psalm 139:17-18). Thank You, Holy Spirit, for revealing so much wisdom to me, and I ask for anything more of what the Father is showing You right now. Thank You, Father. In Jesus' name, AMEN.

But you have made me as strong as a wild ox. You have anointed me with the finest oil. Psalms 92:10

But he was wounded for our transgressions, he was bruised for our iniquities: the chastisement of our peace was upon him; and with his stripes we are healed. Isaiah 53:5 KJV

God is not man, that he should lie, or a son of man, that he should change his mind. Has he said, and will he not do it? Or has he spoken, and will he not fulfill it? Numbers 23:19 ESV

He said, "Daniel, you who are highly esteemed, consider carefully the words I am about to speak to you, and stand up, for I have now been sent to you." And when he said this to me, I stood up trembling. Daniel 10:11 NIV

How precious are your thoughts about me, O God. They cannot be numbered! I can't even count them; they outnumber the grains of sand! And when I wake up, you are still with me! Psalms 139:17-18

To Not Compare Myself with Others:

July 30, 2020

Comparison... How do you avoid it? Comparison seems to be something we do without even thinking. Throughout all the stories in the Bible, comparisons popped up and led to devastating outcomes. The first comparison was in the garden when Adam and Eve compared God's truth with a lie and chose the lie instead (Genesis 3:6). Cain compared his gift to Abel's and felt insecure and angry, leading Cain to later kill Abel (Genesis 4:8). Leah and Rachel had a straight up "birth off" having children to see who Jacob would love more (Genesis 30). Comparison can lead you into making crazy choices. Comparison can cause you to ask questions and worder about your own calling.

Side Note: Before I talk about comparison, I am referring to the type that makes one jealous or in a negative sense. It is not wrong to see qualities or things that you hope to attain one day for you to work on.

This is my confession time. I sometimes look at people in the body of Christ, and I get jealous. Yup, I admit it. It is like the stage just makes their light shine so much brighter than mine. But I am asked this question by Holy Spirit, "Are you supposed to shine to outshine your brothers and sisters or shine brighter to expose the world's darkness?" Comparison seems to be one of the challenges in the body of Christ. We are one body. However, sometimes our finger points to our foot, and then the mouth comes in only to speak the offense between the finger and the foot. We are all connected, but it is like we treat each other as though we are separate. Paul said in 1 Corinthians 12:20 that, "Yes, there are many parts, but only one body." We are now one. The body of Christ was made to carry out the Word to set people free, not to memorize to condemn someone, especially our own brother and sister.

Every time we read about someone in the Bible questioning someone else's identity, it is always exposed as insecurity. Saul, the former king of Israel, is a perfect example of this. It only took one song to trigger Saul.

This was their song: "Saul has killed his thousands, and David his ten thousands!" 1 Samuel 18:7

This made Saul very angry. "What's this?" he said. "They credit David with ten thousands and me with only thousands. Next they'll be making him their king!" So from that time on Saul kept a jealous eye on David. 1 Samuel 18:8-9

I just want to reflect on Saul's logic for a minute because I feel like we might catch ourselves reflecting on this from time to time. Saul was belittling a thousand enemies he had killed. Saul had gotten a thousand of God's people's enemies and taken them out; God would have received glory for even just one. Saul belittled the blessing from God of having the gift, wisdom, and anointing to get rid of God's people's enemies when someone else with their ten thousands was thrown into the mix. Also, the fact that it was David who was anointed to be the next king of Israel probably reminded Saul that his time was short as king as he had done some previous things that cost him his anointing. We are each anointed and have gifts the Holy Spirit gives us, and instead of using them to one-up each other, let us be one and come up higher for Christ. It is not a competition; it is a commission. We need what everybody has been given! People who do not know Jesus Christ as their personal Lord and Savior need us to be one! Jesus needs us to be one!

This story of Saul being jealous of David only happened because, in 1 Samuel chapter 8, the Israelites saw other nations and wanted a king. God knew they would regret this, but they did not heed his warning and got what comparison made them lust for. Comparison can become an unnecessary obstacle in accepting our calling and gifts. We know God has a plan for each of us, but we get caught up in looking at someone else's life. Here are some questions that are from and can lead to comparison:

Why do other people get life so easy, and my life is hard?

I have been praying for something for years, and someone else gets it in minutes without praying.

Why were they healed of cancer, and the person I prayed for was not?

Let me say this. God is not afraid of our questions, but how many of the questions that we are seeking answers to are asked out of fear that stems from doubt, insecurity, shame, or lack of trust in who God says He is and who He says we are in His Word?

How many questions about our calling come

from feeling like the calling we are pretty sure we have is little in comparison to someone else's? A lot of times, we know the answer to our questions. There are times when we do not, but other times, we know the answer and do not want it because it was not the answer we wanted or expected. We built up the hope and space to receive the answer that would stretch our understanding, and then God stretched us even more. We are called to be a leader, but we are not the best at speaking (Moses, Exodus 4:10). There are other people who, when comparing them to yourself, they seem better equipped. God does not compare you to anyone except his Son. When God looks at you, He sees the love, the purity, the righteousness, the wisdom, and everything Jesus died and rose again for us to receive. Yes, God loves everyone. Remember, also, God loves you. God has a plan for you. God thinks highly about you. God protects you. God is for you. You do not need to compare yourself to anyone except Jesus Christ (this is one of the positive points of comparison in order to inspire us). What God has for you will meet and surpass the desires of your heart.

How do you avoid the trap of comparison? First off, traps are set along paths that an animal takes consistently and usually have what the animal likes to eat or draws their interest in far enough to set it off. Some traps are very inconspicuous in their appearance. The traps set by the enemy fall in line with how trappers set their traps for animals. Comparison is going to be more than likely along a path, thinking, or things you see daily.

Example: You want to be seen as important (bait), but your gift does not have a stage for it to be showcased (insecurity does not come from God; just remember who bred insecurity). You get a little jealous, and then it turns into burning jealousy, which becomes anger, and then this leads to slander (cage), and pretty soon, your gift is wasted while you try to hinder someone else's gift from being seen by tearing them down (door is closed and locked).

When you find this trap, it will draw you in and get your attention. Once you are in the trap, it is hard to get out on your own, but thankfully, Jesus has the key to the house of David found in Isaiah 22:22, which is *"the highest position in the royal court. When he opens doors, no one will be able to close them; when he closes doors, no one will be able to open them."*

I hinted earlier in this chapter that there are some questions that pop up that open the door to comparison. I know a recent example, so recent that it is happening as I write this book. Will this be a good enough book? Does it have enough pages? Are the things I am talking about as good as other writers? Should I even publish this book? Is this even enough to be a book? I am comparing something God has given me to write with every other book that has ever been written. That is a lot of pressure. I am no C.S. Lewis, but that does not mean I should not write what God has given me.

I made the comment that it seems as though, as Christians, we struggle with comparison. It seems weird, considering Jesus is our personal Savior, and we are united in Christ. We know our value and yet constantly try to outshine each other. We have each been given different gifts, and some are more in people's faces to see, while others' gifts are given and a lot of people do not see. I think the key to avoiding comparison and getting out of the trap of it is to believe God sees you. Every day of your life was written about you before you were born (Psalm 139:16). God loves the story He wrote about you and even delights in it. It may not seem like a lot to you, but it is precious to God because you are precious to God. What you do matters to God, but He loves you for you. God loves the plans He has for you, and they are good. When there is a chance to compare, remember who you are, who God says you are, and remember He has a plan for you. You are special to God. You are valuable and precious to him.

For I know the plans I have for you," says the LORD. "They are plans for good and not for disaster, to give you a future and a hope." Jeremiah 29:11

In fact, some parts of the body that seem weakest and least important are actually the most necessary. 1 Cor. 12:22

But our bodies have many parts, and God has put each part just where he wants it. 1 Cor. 12:18

The Prayer List

Prayer:

Father, thank You for today. Today, I ask You for what You have put in my heart. What is my purpose? What is my calling? Holy Spirit, I ask for wisdom and discernment, knowing You give both freely (James 1:5) because of my Lord and Savior, Jesus Christ. Thank You, Father, that when I pray, You will answer (Isaiah 65:24). Let me be sensitive to what You are going to say and how You are going to say it. Thank You for making me and giving me a purpose. Thank You for blessing others, but thank You that You bless me as well (Psalms 31:19). I love You and live to honor You and bring You glory. In Jesus' name, AMEN.

If you need wisdom, ask our generous God, and he will give it to you. He will not rebuke you for asking. James 1:5

I will answer them before they even call to me. While they are still talking about their needs, I will go ahead and answer their prayers! Isaiah 65:24

How great is the goodness you have stored up for those who fear you. You lavish it on those who come to you for protection, blessing them before the watching world. Psalms 31:19

The Prayer List

Renewed Mindset:

July 31, 2020

This prayer request turned into my favorite one to pray for! At first, I was like, 1 Corinthians 2:16, *"We have the mind of Christ,"* and I did not know where to go from there. We renew our minds daily, but I wanted to find other verses than just the same ones we use to renew our minds. I mean, there are amazing verses in the Bible that are not on a t-shirt but are filled with the breath of the Holy Spirit, just waiting to help us on our journey and blow us away!

The verse I was led to by the Holy Spirit is Romans 12:2, which says: *"Don't copy the behavior and customs of this world, but let God transform you into a new person by changing the way you think. Then you will learn to know God's will for you, which is good and pleasing and perfect."* Let us break this down to renew our minds.

Don't copy the ways and customs of this world, but let God transform you into a new person by changing the way you think.

Go ahead and underline or highlight in your mind or in this book, "let God transform you." The first step of renewing [receiving, attaining] your mind is getting rid [throw out, do not let enter] of the ways and customs of this world. Next, you let God transform you. Hold up, let God? You mean it is not in my own strength or understanding I renew my mind!? What? I receive renewing? What? You mean I let God? YES! This was probably why this prayer request became my favorite! It is my favorite because when I hear we need to renew our minds, I picture myself renewing it.

That is fine; we are cal ed to seek God and study His Word. But we are not supposed to do all the work by ourselves. There are callings we cannot fulfill on our own. There are promises we cannot receive on our own apart from God working in our lives. A renewed mindset is one of those promises and callings that we need to do our best and create an atmosphere to receive, but let God do the rest. Let God bring the gift and show you how it works. When you get rid of the thinking that it is up to you to renew your mind in your own strength and instead do what God is asking you to do, you get to receive what God has for you. When your mind is uncluttered with statistics, opinions, and quotes of the world (have no Scripture or utterance of truth based on the Word in them) that have no power to make you into a new person, a space begins to open for God to come in with his Word and Spirit. God will come in because it is the principle of this promise in Romans 12:2 that all you need to do is get rid of the customs and old ways of thinking, then let God.

Side note celebration: Wanting a renewed mind is a good sign, since the old you would not have even known that your mind needed new thinking in the first place.

Another thing to get excited about is that renewing your mind is not a do-it-yourself project. Part of renewing your mind, like I have been trying to convey, is getting rid of the idea that you can do it in your own strength, apart from the one who created your mind and knows every little detail about it. The second part of renewing your mind is getting rid of the thoughts that say, "It is too hard," "You are too stuck in old mindsets," "Too this and too that," "This is how my parents thought," "This is this," and "This is that." The "this" and "too" in the previous phrases are old thinking. In your own strength, the old seems stuck, but once you start pulling them out of your mind, a strength that comes with this promise in Romans 12:2 comes in and lets God do what you could not do. Now, you have a space of hope that you are never too far gone, no matter how long you have had a previous thought. Now, that thought is under the authority of Jesus. Amen.

We destroy every proud obstacle that keeps people from knowing God. We capture their rebellious thoughts and teach them to obey Christ. And after you have become fully obedient, we will punish everyone who remains disobedient. 2 Corinthian 10:5-6

Think of renewing your mind as a treasure hunt. The Holy Spirit is your guide, and the Word is your map. Jesus is the path, and the Father's commands, just like Proverbs 7:1 says, are the treasure. These commands are going to crown your mind with beautiful jewels to replace the fool's gold the world gave you. On a treasure hunt, you might run into pirates trying to take things that are not theirs. They are after your treasure not to benefit from it, but so you will not. There is also much vegetation that needs to be cut away so you can see the next step to take in pursuit of this treasure. And, in Ephesians 6:17, it says you have the sword of the Spirit, which is the Word as our sword, so you use the Word to cut away these leaves trying to disrupt your view and journey, trying to discourage you into settling for the trash of the world and not the treasure of the Father.

It is an adventure! An adventure of a lifetime! What is even more exciting about this adventure is that the Father sees you, gives you pieces of this treasure, and goes ahead of you to help you on the path you are on! *"Do not be afraid or discouraged, for the LORD will personally go ahead of you. He will be with you; he will neither fail you nor abandon you" (Deut. 31:8).* Jesus has walked this path, but the brush still tries to grow, and pirates still try to come, but the Father sees you and is right there with you. You will find the treasure!

If you look for me wholeheartedly, you will find me. Jeremiah 29:13

Another way to look at your mind being renewed is to imagine that God told you He wants to come in and redecorate and refurbish your house with upgrades to anything that is old and restore anything that has been left broken or undone. The part we are called to do is to make room. This seems to be the calling in every area of our lives as Christians, but it is especially important when renewing your mind. Make room, so get rid of some of the old things or clutter in your mind that God wants to upgrade and restore. If the items are too heavy to lift on your own, God has a great moving company that is able to even roll stones away!

On the way they were asking each other, "Who will roll away the stone for us from the entrance to the tomb? But as they arrived, they looked up and saw that the stone, which was very large, had already been rolled aside. Mark 16:3-4

Once you get your mind cleared of the world's customs, God brings the upgrade and restoration to each thought and even shows you how to use the new upgrades and little perks no one else knows about. If you do not know exactly what God wants to upgrade or restore, ask Him. God absolutely adores talking to you about the news He wants to bring and help you with! God loves you so much! Jesus loves you so much! The Holy Spirit loves you so much! You have upgrades in your mind that God is ready to give you, and you have memories He is ready to restore! Yay!

The last thing I want to tell you about a renewed mindset is that it is an ongoing process. I know as a person who likes to complete things and checks things off my list as I do so, this can be challenging as it causes you to shift from your timing and routine to God's ways and rhythm. It will cause you to change your mind about how you look at "process." The world's outlook on the process is negative and does not allow respect, patience, kindness, or any positivity. The Word's outlook on the process is a journey with the One who made you, calls you, and sees you beyond what you are going through.

The new thinking you can receive from God about the process is that it is the chance to get better, freer, purer, wiser, and so much more all the time. You are constantly being filled with blessings, lacking no good thing at any time of your life, including right now. Get in the Word so that it can get inside of you!

Prayer:

Thank You, Father, for renewing my mind. Thank You that it is not all up to me. Thank You for helping and giving me grace through the awesome process of renewing my mind. Thank You that wrong, old thoughts that do not bring life are gone and are ready for upgrade and restoration in Jesus' name, AMEN.

For the LORD God is our sun and our shield. He gives us grace and glory. The LORD will withhold no good thing from those who do what is right. Psalms 84:11

*F*inancial:

August 4, 2020

Finances - this word can trigger different responses. Some people's finances are good and do not keep them up at night, others experience the complete opposite. Your finances have every chance to stress you out since your financial situation can change within a second. Proverbs 23:4-5 sums it up best, *"Don't wear yourself out trying to get rich. Be wise enough to know when to quit. In the blink of an eye, wealth disappears, for it will sprout wings and fly away like an eagle."* With the stress of finances comes fear and wondering why. To be honest with you, I am still learning about this topic. But what I do know is we have been given different ways of provision; my finances may look different than yours. There may be times when God is calling me to give more than what I budgeted for, but

God is not calling us to live in poverty. His Kingdom is already funded with His provision; all we have to do is ask, receive, believe, and use our citizenship in the Kingdom of Heaven.

Financial peace is going to look different for everyone. For some, $100 is like a $1,000 in value, and for others, $100 is like a $1 value. We each have different responsibilities with talents and money. We keep searching for the secret recipe for peace in our finances when there are principles in the Bible that can teach you how to be prosperous no matter what ingredients you have. Money changes, but God does not. God wants what you have now, not to bankrupt you, but to show you that when you give Him what you have and do your best, He will take care of the rest. The more you depend on anything but God and go about it without the wisdom and discernment that comes from the Word of God, the more confused you will be when it comes to things like money.

I sense Holy Spirit wants me to also talk about how you can have great finances and be rich, but this does not always mean you know God. What do you mean? Well, let me ask you this: what would make you rich? Let me ask you another question: why do you want to be rich? See, prosperity is a biblical principle, but it is not limited to money. The prosperity God's people receive is not reliant on money; it is reliant on God, our provider. Now, I am not saying you need to go bankrupt for the Lord or view money as a sign that you are evil. What I am saying is if money is the one you are serving and fearing, you need to repent and remember the One who has given you money; your love should be for Him alone. We do not depend on money; we depend on God. We do not depend on what is provided; we depend on the provider. We trust what God does, but even more, we trust who He is with whatever we have. When our hearts pursue righteousness, we will find life, righteousness, and honor (Proverbs 21:21).

Look at the *"Parable of the Three Servants"* in *"Again, the Kingdom of Heaven can be illustrated by the story of a man going on a long trip. He called together his servants and entrusted his money to them while he was gone. He gave five bags of silver to one, two bags of silver to another, and one bag of silver to the last- dividing it in proportion to their abilities. He then left on his trip. The servant who received the five bags of silver began to invest the money and earned five more. The servant with two bags of silver also went to work and earned two more. But the servant who received one bag of silver dug a hole in the ground and hid the master's money. (Matthew 25:14-18).*

The servant with five and two bags of silver

explained to the master how they had taken what he had left them and invested and earned more. In both cases, the master said, *"Well done my good and faithful servant. You have been faithful in handling this small amount, so now I will give you many more responsibilities. Let's celebrate together!" (Matthew 25:21,23)* The servant who did nothing explained that the master was unpredictable and basically did not truly know the master at all and not only did nothing with the money but buried it where no one, not even the master, experienced some type of increase in the return of what was given.

You may be picking up on the fact that this is not just about money, and you are right. This story is another parable used to explain the Kingdom of God and what it is like. I used this story because you are so much more than your financial situation. You have money, but you also have talents and gifts God has given you to expand and increase His Kingdom here on earth. You see, we do not know when God, our master, will come back, but He is.

Jesus is coming back soon. When Jesus comes back, he exceeds our expectations time and time again. Use what God has given you. This is not limited to money; to think you are only a bank account to God is a lie from Hell. You are a child of the Most High God. You are valuable. You have something (s) God has given you for such a time as this (Esther 4:14). I mean, I did not think I would be writing a book, but the more I put what God has given me together, low and behold my notes from my composition book grew into a full-on book. What do you have pieces of that God wants you to invest into His Kingdom which is all around you? God has placed His Kingdom within you; you have things deposited in you from God, so when you want to make the transfer, go to the note of the Word and call it out. Whatever you need is in there! Use them well so we can all celebrate with God and be called his good and faithful servants. Amen.

Neither shall they say, Lo here! Or lo there! for, behold, the kingdom of God is within you. Luke 17:21 KJV

I will leave you with these final thoughts and a Bible verse to think about and give you an idea to take you into some time with the Holy Spirit:

» Some people have money and serve God. Other people have God and serve money.

» Some people have talents and serve God. Other people have God and serve talents.

» Some people have it all and serve God. Other people have God and serve it all.

They traded the truth about God for a lie. So they worshipped and served the things God created instead of the Creator himself, who is worthy of eternal praise! Amen. Romans 1:25

Prayer:

Father, thank You that Your Kingdom is not one of just a lot of talk; it is one of power (1 Cor. 4:20). Thank You, your Word will not come back void (Isaiah 55:11, AMP). It is in Your word [that will not come back void] You said, "You have not because you ask not." Father, I am asking for financial peace in MY finances. Thank You, we have peace past understanding (Phil. 4:7). Thank You that You do not call us to live in poverty. Poverty is a curse and the result of not being obedient or faithful with what You have given us. Thank You that You have set me free from my inadequacies and sin, and I am a new creation free from condemnation (Romans 8:1). I repent of the times I was not a good steward of what You gave me. The money I have wasted, talent, time, resources, people, and any other gift You have given me that I was not obedient to You or faithful to You in. I come to You confessing my sin, and I am grateful to ask and receive Your forgiveness for it. Holy Spirit, if there is anything else I need to repent of, show me. Anything in my heart that offends You, Lord, show me (Psalms 139:24). In Jesus' name, AMEN.

For the Kingdom of God is not just a lot of talk; it is living by God's power. 1 Cor. 4:20

So will My word be which goes out of My mouth; It will not return to Me void (useless, without result), Without accomplishing what I desire, And without succeeding in the matter for which I sent it. Isaiah 55:11 AMP

Then you will experience God's peace, which exceeds anything we can understand. His peace will guard your hearts and minds as you live in Christ Jesus. Phil. 4:7

So now there is no condemnation for those who belong to Christ Jesus. Romans 8:1

Point out anything in me that offends you, and lead me along the path of everlasting life. Psalms 139:24

*T*o See Myself and Others the Way Jesus Does:

August 6, 2020, August 10, 2020

There is a special blessing that comes from seeing and hearing people with eyes to see and ears to hear. When you love people with the heart of the Father, it changes you and changes the way you love people. Our love can only go so far, but the love of the Father reaches beyond what we cannot break through. We have this breakthrough blessing available to us. Proverbs 20:12 tells us that *"eyes to see and ears to hear are gifts from the Lord."* Romans 5:5 also tells us that the love of God is in us, and we can know we are loved *"because He has given us the Holy Spirit to fill our hearts with his love."*

A great verse about loving others and ourselves comes from 1 John 4:20:

If someone says, "I love God," but hates a fellow believer, that person is a liar; for if we don't love people we can see, how can we love God, whom we cannot see? And he has given us this command: Those who love God must also love their fellow believers.

Wow! You think you are holy, and then you start thinking about the thoughts and words you have for certain people that you do not like, and your liver starts to quiver. If I could enter a GIF of someone having some regret on their face, I would. The truth is, there are times when we feel as though there is no reason to love someone or see someone the way God sees them because they are making it difficult. It almost feels like a sacrifice. You have to sacrifice your understanding of that person in the moment for what God says about them in His Word. You have to choose to see the person as someone worth dying for because, like you, God loves them. We all have our moments, but God loves us, in each one, 100%.

The saying, "hurt people, hurt people," is an understatement at times. However, we are called to love. The very people Jesus saw as they were being created were the same people who were mocking and looking for Jesus to mess up. The people Jesus came to save ended up nailing Him to the cross. I am not saying we need to stay in abusive relationships at all. The point I make is that, as Christians, we cannot forget what carrying a cross entails. Matthew 16:24 tells us, *"Then Jesus said to his disciples, 'If any of you wants to be my follower, you must give up your own way, take up your cross, and follow me.'"* It is going to mean that people are going to be wrong about you and voice what they think about you while you are being obedient to God. People are going to whip you with their success at times when it looks like you are failing. People are even going to call you out while you are being called by God to carry out the things He set for you to accomplish for Him.

The great thing about carrying a cross is we have Jesus right by our side. It is not a physical cross we carry like Jesus, but one that comes with letting go of the old and entering the new. So yeah, people are going to seem unlovable. However, when you look at the cross, you can remember the act of love that came from the cross Jesus carried before us, which has set us free to be loved and to love. We carry our cross, so we carry forgiveness with us always.

Now, we are in the Kingdom of God, and we get to experience and have the love of God dwell in us. When you take a few seconds and think about how much God loves you, it gets a little easier to love those who seem unlovable. Love is more than a feeling; it is a choice. Your feelings are going to steer you in all kinds of directions, but the Holy Spirit will only lead you into all truth (John 16:13). Remember, you are now a Kingdom person who has value, and no one can take this away from you.

Ill-gotten treasures have no lasting value, but righteousness delivers from death.
Proverbs 10:2 (NIV)

The world gives you every reason to not love someone, to not love yourself. You are too this and too that. Well, the Word of God that has prophecy being fulfilled to this day, possibly one right now at this second, gives you every reason to love other people and love yourself. You are too precious to God to not take part in the gift of sharing his love. You are too valuable to God to miss out on any good thing, including seeing the value in other people given by God.

As previously illustrated, with carrying a cross, there are going to be times when you are being obedient to your Father even though it is uncomfortable, like loving someone who you do not feel deserves love. It means showing someone love, forgiveness, or whatever the Holy Spirit shows you even though they have not shown it to you first. Do not forget the goodness God shows you every day, and remember that as you are a son or a daughter of Christ, so is the person you are tempted to hate. Being in a kingdom means loving everyone in it, especially those everyone else pushes to the side or comes from nothing. I recall an important person coming out of a place where no one believed anything good could come from, wink, wink.

"Nazareth!" exclaimed Nathanael. "Can anything good come from Nazareth?" "Come and see for yourself," Philip replied. John 1:46

Part. 2: When I was writing about this topic, this was towards the end of the thirty days of prayer, and I forgot I had already written about this, but it worked out because the Holy Spirit showed me another way to look at this. The second verse I was led to was 2 Corinthians 4:18 and Isaiah 11:3, which say:

So we don't look at the troubles we can see now; rather, we fix our gaze on things that cannot be seen. For the things we see now will soon be gone, but the things we cannot see will last forever.

He will delight in obeying the LORD. He will not judge by appearance nor make decision based on hearsay.

Looking at other people, we see their clothes, hair, body, eyes, etc. However, eventually, they will buy different clothes, change their hair, get taller or shorter, their minds will change, and so much more will change. If we want to see ourselves and others the way Jesus does, we cannot get so caught up in the moment. Just like God is constantly working in us, filling us up with what we need, He is doing that on the inside of others, too. Try to remember God's work is often unseeab e, but it is undeniable. We did not see how God formed us or how He changed us, but there is no denying He did.

Shift your eyes to an eternal vision; shift where you lay your gaze to f nd love. Like God did when He anointed David in 1 Samuel 16:7, look at the heart. That is where true kings and queens are found. Look at your heart. Proverbs 27:19 says, *"that the heart reflects the true person."* Sometimes, though, when you think about loving others, and try to see beyond the surface, there are wounds from others in your heart that come to the surface. These wounds tend to hold your heart captive so that no love comes in or comes out. Your heart is in survival mode, trying to heal. But Jesus has come to heal the brokenhearted (Luke 4:18). A big part of the healing process, especially when it comes to wounds in your heart, is forgiveness. Ahhh, forgiveness?!?

Yeah, forgiveness. If money does not trigger you, forgiveness might. When you hear preachers preaching on forgiveness, they, at some point, say,

"I am not trying to minimize what happened to you," I say the same thing now. I also ask, though, do you think that when Jesus died on the cross for you, every hurt or sin you would ever experience put on Him, that pain was minimized? No, Jesus felt it completely, but also forgave and healed it completely and offers us the complete gift of forgiveness for ourselves and others. Jesus chose to forgive us, and part of loving other people and ourselves the way Jesus does is to forgive others and ourselves, even when it is the most painful thing at the moment.

> *This High Priest of ours understands our weaknesses, for he faced all of the same testings we do, yet he did not sin. So, let us come boldly to the throne of our gracious God. There, we will receive his mercy, and we will find grace to help us when we need it the most. Hebrews 4:15-16*

Jesus' crucifixion and suffering did not last forever; if we go look at the tomb He laid in, it is still empty. The tomb Jesus was in was borrowed. Just like Jesus, you do not have to stay in someone else's tomb. Just like Lazarus, Jesus is calling you out of there, giving you new clothing, getting rid of the stench of what the world wrapped you in (John 11:43-44). The world trying to save you leads to death as people living according to the world wrapped up Lazarus and rolled the stone to seal his destiny of death. To the crowd, life meant moving on; to Jesus, life meant mcving the stone. Jesus comes to us and rolls the stone away; we trade our bandages of death for balms of forgiveness and redemption fragranced with a perfume of eternal love. Our destiny is now a destiny of life!

Whoever finds his life [in this world] will [eventually] lose it [through death], and whoever loses his life [in this world] for my sake will find it [that is, life with Me for all eternity].
Matthew 10:39 (AMP)

We have been born again by believing in our hearts and confessing with our mouths that Jesus died for our sins. He rose again on the third day with authority and power rightfully restored. Again, just like Jesus is at the right hand of the Father, we are also seated in heavenly p aces (Ephesians 2:6). When you sit close to God, you begin to see others from His perspective, forgiven.

Prayer:

Thank You, Father, for the heart. Thank You for Your heart. Thank You that we can follow Your example of examining people by what is in their hearts. Father, You said, "Just as you can tell a tree by its fruit, we tell a person by their actions." (Matthew 7:20). The heart is truly a reflection of who we are (Proverbs 27:19). Thank You that You change our hearts and fill them up with Your goodness. Thank You for showing us how to love others when we have no reason to. You are the reason why we love. You are love (1 John 4:8). Thank You; love is not limited to certain people. You poured out Your love for everyone (John 3:16). Let us walk with this kind of love now. In Jesus' name, AMEN.

Yes, just as you can identify a tree by its fruit, so you can identify people by their actions. Matthew 7:20

As a face is reflected in water, so the heart reflects the real person. Proverbs 27:19

But anyone who does not love does not know God, for God is love. 1 John 4:8

"For this is how God loved the world: He gave his one and only Son, so that everyone who

believes in him will not perish but have eternal life." John 3:16

*F*reedom from Any Doubt:

August 11, 2020

Doubt has a way of taking over our faith. Doubt shouts over the gentle whisper of God's voice. Since doubt is louder at times than faith, we step back into the trap of doubt. Doubt will never set you free from anything, so why do we run to something that would hinder us? The reason why I fall into doubt is because it is a familiar path to me. We are a new creation, but some of us are wearing the same shoes. The shoes that we walked in before we were born again came worn out, and that is the way they always looked since you had no hope. Now we have the shoes of the Gospel of Peace (Ephesians 6:15). You can have peace wherever you go. You are standing on peace, which leads you to the path of faith. Do not try to put on the old doubt shoes over your peace shoes, or else you will be uncomfortable and will not want to walk out what Jesus has for you.

We are free. We are free from sin. We are free from our past. We are free from doubt. We know the truth about who we are. The moment we take on any other definition of who we are that is not rooted in the Word, the door opens to forget, which leads me to the two verses to claim for this prayer request.

So Christ has truly set us free. Now make sure that you stay free, and don't get tied up again in the slavery to the law. Galatians 5:1

For you have been called to live in freedom, my brothers and sisters. But don't use your freedom to satisfy your sinful nature. Instead, use your freedom to serve one another in love. Galatians 5:13

When you first receive Jesus into your heart, it is as if you are on fire for all His promises and commands. But, just as a candle is running out of its wick, we no longer have anything to light. We let days filled with God's promises for us go by. Why? When you don't use something for a while, you can forget about it. It is the same thing with freedom from God. Galatians 5 reminds us you are free, but make sure you stay that way. Reminding yourself

that you are free is a great way not to forget.
You can know that you are free from doubt because you are free from anything that would try to take you out of God's will. The Holy Spirit is also a great reminder that you are free. Doubt is uncertainty and lack of conviction, but the Holy Spirit gives us confidence and convicts/convinces us in our troubles that we can believe God is for us and has plans to give us a hope and a future. Jesus said,

But when the Father sends the Advocate as my representative- that is, the Holy Spirit- he will teach you everything and will remind you of everything I have told you. John 14:26

Doubt is very sneaky and blunt at the same time. It is sneaky because it finds areas in our thinking that are weak to attack. It is blunt because once it finds this area, it acts like it is the king and the master. This whole book is about finding examples in the Bible that give insight into how other people got their answers. A great example of doubt that shows its sneakiness and bluntness is in Exodus 14. The way the story starts out is the Lord instructing Moses to order the Israelites to turn back, so that they would camp between Migdal and the sea. In other words, God wanted his people to be in a place at that time between where they had been and could not go back because of what God had done for them.

At the same time, the Israelites were also between the sea where they were going but could not go without God and only because of God. Confused? It says God wanted to confuse Pharaoh by making him think that the Israelites were confused. God wanted Pharaoh to think they were trapped, which would already add a few more drops to his arrogantly flooded heart to chase after the Israelites.

Wait, what? God causing the enemy to chase after His people? Always make sure to read the whole story of the Bible because the story in its entirety is the best part! God wanted Pharaoh to think the Israelites were trapped because God wanted every single one of the Israelites to see the glory of God, and with how hard-hearted Pharaoh was, he was the perfect candidate. Now, you and I know this, and if you read this story, it is like Moses and God had a sneak peek of the movie, but the Israelites did not. They were camping, and Pharaoh changed his mind. The Israelites looked up to see not only Pharaoh but the best of the best of Egypt and everything else Egypt could come up with to attack them, heading straight toward them.

This is where doubt came in and did the only damage to the Israelites. Within only two verses in this story, they began to question everything and wanted to be *"a slave in Egypt rather than a corpse in the wilderness."* (Exodus 14:12). They would have rather live chained than die free.

Doubt questions freedom, especially the freedom God wants to give you in your life. It makes you question everything God did for you, even though you know the answer: God did move in your life. I love the answer God gave Moses, though, and I think it is as applicable today as it was then.

Don't be afraid. Just stand still and watch the Lord rescue you today. The Egyptians you see today will never be seen again. The LORD himself will fight for you. Just stay calm. Exodus 14:13-14

I love that. Just stay calm. I also love how there are no commas between these sentences in this translation, only periods. A period stops a sentence and delivers what the person intends to say. There is nothing to add to what has already been said. God says to you when you face any and every doubt, and you can wield the Sword of the Spirit of Truth (Ephesians 6:17) along with Him right now, "Do not be afraid. Just stand still and watch the Lord rescue you today. The past enemies in every area of your life you see today will never be seen again. The Lord himself will fight for you. Just stay calm." Amen.

Anytime doubt starts to creep in, I encourage you to remember this story. Doubt tried to steal where the Israelites were going. Do not miss out on the miracle just because you cannot see it. Seas were created by God to part; this is God's glory. Enemies (our fight is not against people like in Moses' day, but in a realm, we cannot see) you see today were made to never be a thought in your future. You will have your vision fixed on a higher level than your eye level when you look to God as you help.

For we are not fighting against flesh-and-blood enemies, but against evil rulers and authorities of the unseen world, against mighty powers in this dark world, and against evil spirits in the heavenly places. Ephesians 6:12

I look up to the mountains- does my help come from there? My help comes from the LORD, who made heaven and earth. Psalms 121:1-2

The Prayer List

Prayer:

Woohoo! Father, thank You for freedom from doubt. Thank You for giving me a sound mind with peace, love, and power (2 Timothy 1:7)! Thank You; I do not have to run back when things are against me. Thank You, though the waters flow one way, You give me the strength to go Your way (Isaiah 43:2). Yahweh! Thank You, Holy Spirit, for the revelation and wisdom You are now revealing to me RIGHT NOW! In Jesus' name, AMEN.

For God has not given us a spirit of fear and timidity, but of power, love, and self-discipline. 2 Timothy 1:7

When you go through deep waters, I will be with you. When you go through rivers of difficulty, you will not drown. When you walk through the fire of oppression, you will not be burned up; the flames will not consume you. Isaiah 43:2

Be on guard. Stand firm in the faith. Be courageous. Be strong. 1 Cor. 16:13

*L*ove God, Jesus, and the Holy Spirit Wholeheartedly:

August 12, 2020

In searching for ways to love God, Jesus, and Holy Spirit, obedience was a common factor. In 1 John 5:3, it says, *"Loving God means keeping his commandments, and his commandments are not burdensome."* In John 14:15, it says, *"If you love me, obey my commandments."* And again, in John 15:10, it says, *"When you obey my commandments, you remain in my love, just as I obey my Father's commandments and remain in his love."* Obedience does not have to take on the negative connotation the world gives it. Obedience can be a gift in disguise that helps you start understanding the Father more. When you understand the Father more, there will be even more love for Him and yourself.

It is kind of crazy how God's version of loving Him is obedience when we think the way we love God is by being perfect. We think if we pray and read the same verse exactly a set number of times, we are loving God. God's love does not require things like we require things. God's love requires our trust and obedience in that the One who made you knows you and wants you to be victorious. The way we love God is by storing His commands in our hearts and learning through obedience why His commands are so important. God wants us to obey Him because He can obey and carry His word out, which blesses you when you are obedient to what He has commanded.

Yes, Adam's one sin brings condemnation for everyone, but Christ's one act of righteousness brings a right relationship with God and new life for everyone.

Because one person disobeyed God, many became sinners. But because one other person obeyed God, many will be made righteous. Romans 5:18-19

We learn that the very commands God wants us to store in our hearts keep us safe and give us life, joy, faith, hope, gentleness, patience, comfort, peace, and every promise ever made by God. What commands are you not storing in your heart?

We know about commandments and obedience, but like Saul, we think sacrifice is more important. It is in 1 Samuel 15, when Saul was the current king of Israel that we dive into our story. When talking about obedience, there were countless times Saul was not obedient and instead did what he thought was right instead of what God told him was right. God told Samuel, the prophet, to tell Saul God was ready to settle the accounts with the nation of Amalek for opposing Israel when they came from Egypt. Saul was instructed to completely destroy the Amalek nation; nothing be left of it. Saul got the army together and did destroy the Amalekites.

Saul did not completely obey what God had said, though. God said destroy them completely. Saul captured the Amalekite king, Agag, and spared the best of the sheep, cattle, fat calves, goats, and lambs. Before we continue in this story, out of all the things to spare, Saul spared a king. Saul spared the best of what the Amalekites had. In other words, he spared a ruler and his assets. I just had to get that out of the way. The next part of the story, in verse nine, said that Saul and his men were *"sparing everything, in fact, that appealed to them."* The best of what God told you to get rid of is still a command from God to get rid of it. Ask the

Holy Spirit what this means; it is not as literal as we think. God commands us to get rid of the customs of the world (Romans 12:2), but we decide to take the best of what it has to offer, the appealing parts, and say I am so obedient to the Lord, though. I should build something for myself or share a picture of how obedient I am so all can see. Saul did this, too; it was when Samuel came to tell Saul how he had disobeyed God in verse twelve that Saul was setting up a monument for himself. Wow, ouch!

You are chosen by God but still feel insecure?! You have been given the command to let go of the past and receive God's restoration of it, but only let go of the bad and keep the good? Jesus has come to make you completely new. Even holding onto the good that Jesus is ready to make even better can be disobedience. Believe me, the previous sentence made me a little shaken as well. Get rid of the good? Before any hasty decisions are made, let us be mature Christians right now. You and I both know that what the good in the story about Saul that he did not spare were goods from another nation that did anything and everything to oppress the people of God at a vulnerable time (and again, our fight is not with people, but of principalities). Do not forget God's goodness, but when He tells you there is an upgrade, something he wants to restore in your life, let Him. Even blooms have to be cut off to grow stronger and last longer. It is not easy to hear; imagine writing it. In the pruning seasons, where even blooms have to be picked, you see what was good be purposely picked off.

It is easy to feel sad about what is gone, but take it from someone who has had to pick hundreds of blooms off of petunias: the new blooms are brighter, stronger, and bigger. The blooms that were easy to pick had this sound of letting go that brought me so much peace, while the ones that were tougher just made the whole process harder than it needed to be.

Saul was commanded to let go of the past nation that hurt Israel; Saul wanted to hold on. God wanted Saul to hold onto what God commanded, but Saul held onto what he saw (hmm, Saul saw). I think how we can compare to Saul as God commands us to let go of the old thoughts, patterns, and areas of our lives that opposed us stepping into the destiny He has for us. God now wants you to hold onto Jesus and the new He offers you every day. This hold is challenged when we see some of the things the world does in life that are appealing and "not so bad" and because we settle there, we stand before the Lord with less than what he already gave everything for us to have. There is a peace like the sound of a petunia's bloom, letting go to grow a new one about being obedient in letting go of holding on to something God wants to restore and settle the account with.

Live in obedience, and you will live in God's love. When you begin to acknowledge and let go of things holding you back, spaces will start to open up in your heart to love God, Jesus, and the Holy Spirit wholeheartedly.

Prayer:

Holy Spirit, we ask You right now to reveal any commands that we are not storing in our hearts and, therefore, leave a door open to sin against God. Reveal to us the commands we need. Holy Spirit help us to take delight in God's discipline and Word (Psalms 119:47). Guide us to the verses that will be what we need (Proverbs 22:18). Help us love You with Your Word and our hearts. In Jesus' name (John 14:21), AMEN.

How I delight in your commands! How I love them! Psalms 119:47

For it is good to keep these sayings in your heart and always ready on your lips. Proverbs 22:18

Those who accept my commandments and obey them are the ones who love me. And because they love me, my Father will love them. And I will love them and reveal myself to each of them." John 14:21

Be the Hands and Feet of Jesus:

August 12, 2020, August 19, 2020

If we were to look at a map of where Jesus' hands and feet went, would it be where we were expecting? Would Jesus' hands and feet have stayed in the religious hot spot of Jerusalem and made the occasional stop to his hometown, Nazareth? Would Jesus go where people expected the Messiah to go? I do not have an exact map of Jesus' journey, but I do know from the stories in the Bible that Jesus went to places that religion would not even talk about. Jesus let his feet cross both physical and spiritual barriers that religious leaders built, not God. The hands and feet of Jesus are gentle but, at the same time, strong and mighty.

Stretch out your hand with healing power; may miraculous signs and wonders be done through the name of your holy servant Jesus. Acts of the Apostles 4:30

The LORD said to my Lord, "Sit in the place of honor at my right hand until I humble your enemies, making them a footstool under your feet." Psalms 110:1

To be the hands and feet of Jesus first requires us to receive the healing and steps toward the Father they took for us. Also, the hands and feet of Jesus went to places that a religious spirit would not take you.

In order for our natural hands and feet to work, they are connected to several systems that relay back and forth what the hands and feet are trying to accomplish. It is a similar concept when we want to be the hands and feet of Jesus. We must receive the Holy Spirit that relays purpose to our hands and feet. The Holy Spirit releases the wisdom from God about His Kingdom and revelation of this wisdom of why He created our hands and feet to serve in His Kingdom.

It all starts with Jesus. Get to know Jesus; I guarantee that if you have known Jesus all your life, there is something new to learn about Him. Once you receive one revelation about Jesus there is another one and another one, and it keeps on going. Reaching, grabbing, and stepping where Jesus calls you is amazing and a great thing to ask for. Recognizing we need this guidance is a big step in itself. The more you know about what the hands and feet of Jesus have accomplished for you is, a great start to discover how to be the ambassador He has called you to be.

So we are Christ's ambassadors; God is making his appeal through us. We speak for Christ when we plead, "Come back to God!" 2 Cor. 5:20

As believers, when we hear about being the hands and feet of Jesus, sometimes a religious spirit tries to disqualify us. How can you be the hands and feet of Jesus? Look what you did yesterday. You still struggle with this. Blah, blah, blah! You are made righteous and clean through the Blood of Jesus Christ. Perfection is not required to be the hands and feet of Jesus; purity that could only come by the precious Holy Spirit is. Wash your hands in the Word and be made clean by the Blood of Jesus Christ. Receive the purity and strength from Jesus. Jesus will lead you in the right direction to reach people. Before you can reach, though, you need to reach out to the one who says, come.

Come close to God, and God will come close to you. Wash your hands, you sinners; purify your hearts, for your loyalty is divided between God and the world. James 4:3

"Yes, come," Jesus said. So Peter went over the side of the boat and walked on the water toward Jesus. Matthew 14:29

Part 2: This was another thing Holy Spirit showed me about Jesus' hands and feet. While there is an infinite amount of verses that talk about the love and service of Jesus' hands and feet, there is another thing the hands and feet of Jesus did. Here is the Scripture that demonstrates the hope in the hands and feet of Jesus:

But when he saw the strong winds and waves, he was terrified and began to sink. "Save me Lord," he shouted. Jesus immediately reached out and grabbed him. Matthew 14:30-31

Jesus' hands and feet touched impossible situations in obedience and love for the Father. Another example of this is when Jesus' hands and feet were pierced. The point I make with this is that Jesus' hands and feet were and are still the hope in hopeless situations.

If you want to be the hands and feet of Jesus, long for His heart. As we learned in previous chapters, the heart reflects the person. Think about all the people Jesus talked to, hung out with, healed, revealed himself as the Messiah to, and ultimately changed their lives. Some of them were high up according to that time period, but most were the average, poor, despised, no one anyone would want to be around on accident, and Jesus was there on purpose just for them.

"The Spirit of the LORD is upon me, for he has anointed me to bring Good News to the poor. He has sent me to proclaim that captives will be released, that the blind will see, that the oppressed will be set free, and that the time of the LORD's favor has come. Luke 4:18-19

So Jesus explained, "I tell you the truth, the Son can do nothing by himself. He does only what he sees the Father doing. Whatever the Father does, the Son also does. John 5:19-20

Jesus did what He saw His Father doing. His Father was healing people, setting them free, reminding them of who they really are, who they were always meant to be, and how God saw them. When Jesus saw someone struggling, I have to believe the Father showed Jesus that person through the Father's eyes and saw the Father's heart overflowing with compassion like in Luke 7:13, *"When the Lord saw her, his heart overflowed with compassion. 'Don't cry!' he said."* There was something blocking God's children from experiencing the love of the Father. Think about it. You are a father, but your children do not realize it.

They are blind to seeing you this way. Think about the longing in your heart to step in in any way possible for them to recognize their daddy and how much you love them and want to be in their life.

Jesus' hands and feet are connected and directed by the heart of the Father. Do not get caught up and discouraged if your hands and feet are in hopeless, broken, and painful situations. Remember that because of what Jesus' hands and feet have done for you, you will get through this.

You have hope in a hopeless situation. Jesus unlocked your healing, and like the man with the crippled hand in the Bible, Jesus has healed you so you can do what you could not [hindered, not able, insecure] do before and be the hands and feet of Jesus because your hands and feet are filled with the Spirit of Jesus.

He looked around at them angrily and was deeply saddened by their hard hearts. Then he said to the man, "Hold out your hand." So the man held out his hand, and it was restored! Mark 3:5

When I saw him, I fell at his feet as I were dead. But he laid his right hand on me and said, "Don't be afraid! I am the First and the Last." Rev. 1:17

Prayer:

Jesus, thank You for making me your hands and feet (1 Cor. 12:27). Thank You for what Your hands and feet, with obedience and love to God, accomplished for me (John 5:36). Thank You that wherever I step, I believe I bring hope in a hopeless situation. I know this hope because You brought hope in the most hopeless situation of all, that is, me being a slave to sin. Thank You, Jesus, for setting me free; send me with Your freedom to the nations (1 Cor. 9:19, KJV). In Jesus' name, AMEN.

All of you together are Christ's body, and each of you is a part of it. 1 Cor. 12:27

But I have a greater witness than John- my teachings and my miracles. The Father gave me these works to accomplish, and they prove that he sent me. John 5:36

Jesus replied, "Go tell that fox that I will keep on casting out demons and healing people today and tomorrow; and the third day I will accomplish my purpose. Luke 13:32

For though I be free from all men, yet have I made myself servant unto all, that I might gain the more. 1 Cor. 9:19 KJV

Savanna Watson

To Do Something that Advances God's Kingdom:

August 14, 2020

The Kingdom of God is more than a castle. The Kingdom is filled with land and people. The Kingdom of God is not just business as usual. The Kingdom of God is God's heart for people. The Kingdom of God is not just where people get healed because God is able, but they get healed because God cares about His people and longs to see them whole. When we share the love of God, we are advancing His Kingdom. When we are obedient, we are advancing God's Kingdom. It is not necessarily about what we do with what the world has given; it is about what we do with what we have received from the Word that shows us how to advance the Kingdom of God.

Here are a few of the words God has given us to grab on and share in His Kingdom:

"God blesses those who are poor and realize their need for him, for the Kingdom of Heaven is theirs. God blesses those who are persecuted [do right even in obedience to God, even though it goes against what everybody in the world is doing] for doing right, for the Kingdom of Heaven is theirs." Matthew 5:3,10 (emphasis added mine)

"Only those who actually do the will of my Father will enter." Matthew 7:21

Jesus is the way! In order to advance the Kingdom, you have to be a part of it, an active member that comes to all the meetings [daily encounters with God through His Word]. Once you receive that and use it, you will get to live your life with the purpose of the Kingdom. Now, when you walk into the store, pull up in the drive-thru, see your neighbor, visit family, or go to work, you have a new purpose. It is not to act religiously but to act on the Word of God and demonstrate its power and authority.

The Word of God is waiting for someone who has been made righteous because of Jesus Christ to use its authority to change things around you and bring in the Kingdom of God. A part of being in the Kingdom of God is using the gifts He has given you. After all, you are now an heir to the inheritance of God (Lamentations 3:24). You have a calling, but just like everything in the Kingdom of God and the basic principle of a kingdom in general, it helps to know the One calling you. There is more guidance and direction that comes with the gift of wisdom of how to build the Kingdom of God when you learn more about the King, Jesus. King Jesus rules and reigns forever!

This chapter is short, but purposely so. You have got the tools. After reading this book, I believe you have practical exercises of your faith to put into your daily routine, even just for a few minutes. Minutes turn into hours, hours into days, days into weeks, weeks into months, months into years, years into decades, and decades into centuries. Do not belittle what a minute seeking God can do in your life. I leave you with these two promises to encourage you and to carry into your life every day.

"Seek the Kingdom of God above all else, and live righteously, and he will give you everything you need." Matthew 6:33

Now may the God of peace- who brought up the dead of our Lord Jesus, the great Shepherd of the sheep, and ratified an eternal covenant with his blood- may he equip you with all you need for doing his will. May he produce in you, through the power of Jesus Christ, every good thing that is pleasing to him. All glory to him forever and ever! Amen. Hebrews 13:20-21

Prayer:

Thank You, Father, for You. Thank You that You are the true representation of pure Holiness (Matthew 6:9). Thank You for bringing Your Kingdom to Earth through Jesus (Luke 17:21). Now that we have the Holy Spirit, we can be led to serve and carry Your Kingdom wherever we go. Father, is there anything hindering me from purely serving Your Kingdom? I ask that You would show me how I can truly be a part of what You want to do, of what You sent me to do (John 17:18). No matter how big or small, You are the God that cares about it all. Thank You for trusting me with the ability to choose you. Thank You that right now, You are downloading the blueprints of Your Kingdom inside of me. You are imparting in me the statement of what your Kingdom stands for. Thank You that no matter where I go or what my thoughts and feelings say, I am in Your Kingdom, and I do have access and the authority to use what You have given because I am now united with Jesus Christ (Ephesians 2:13). Thank You, Father, that You love me and nothing will ever separate me from that (Romans 8:38-39). In Jesus' name, what I am asking is mine by faith, AMEN.

Pray like this: Our Father in heaven, may your

name be kept holy. Matthew 6:9

You won't be able to say, 'Here it is!' or 'It's over there!' For the Kingdom of God is already among you." Luke 17:21

Then he sent them out to tell everyone about the Kingdom of God and to heal the sick. Luke 9:2

Just as you sent me into the world, I am sending them into the world. John 17:18

But now you have been united with Christ Jesus. Once you were far away from God, but now you have been brought near to him through the blood of Christ. Ephesians 2:13

And I am convinced that nothing can separate us from God's love. Neither death nor life, neither angels nor demons, neither our fears for today nor our worries about tomorrow- not even the powers of hell can separate us from God's love. No power in the sky above or in the earth below- indeed, nothing in all creation will ever be able to separate us from the love of God that is revealed in Christ Jesus our Lord. Romans 8:38-39

The End...BUT the Beginning

I hope you enjoyed this little book. I pray that it brought you comfort, and I am confident it did since Scripture gives us comfort and confidence. There were times I was writing this and honestly wondered what it was. However, this is a book! This is Savanna Watson's– daughter of the Most High God, heir to the throne, anointed, set apart, Jesus' sheep, faith-filled, Father-filled, grace ran, truth-abiding child of the Most High God's book. This book is written for you, mom– daughter of the Most High God, one seated in heavenly places with the Father, beautiful, overcoming, secure, confident child of God. This book is also for anyone who reads it. Feel free to fill in your name anywhere you want to receive what the Word has made available through this writing.

The Holy Spirit is also the author of this book since I literally would have no wisdom at all on these topics apart from Him, so balloons and confetti falling everywhere for the Holy Spirit!!! There were so many times I had no idea what I would write next, but as long as I was faithful to type, the Holy Spirit would give me the right words. Thank You, Father, Jesus, and Holy Spirit, for blessing me and anyone who reads this book. In Jesus' name, Amen.

In my own strength, this seemed impossible. But

when I leaned into God and His Word, it became possible. I love you and believe God not only has great plans for you but God also has great plans with you. I will end this book with this:

Here's what Yahweh says to you: "I know all about the marvelous destiny I have in store for you, a future planned out in detail. My intention is not to harm you but to surround you with peace and prosperity and to give you a beautiful future, glistening with hope. Jeremiah 29:11 TPT

Enjoy Jesus. Go write your story with the author and finisher of your faith (Hebrews 12:2, KJV). It's your turn now!

Side note: After this chapter, there is the prayer to accept Jesus as your Lord and Savior. I want to let you know that admitting your sins and turning to someone greater than you, who straight up created this world, is the wisest and best thing you could and will ever do. Jesus is not going to use your sins against you; the exact opposite. Jesus is going to blot them out and use His Word for you!

"I- yes, I alone-will blot out your sins for my own sake and will never think of them again." Isaiah 43:25

Imagine you are looking at this page, and it represents your sins; now close the book. Do you see the page anymore? No. I know the book is still there, but it is impossible to read a book that is closed. Once Jesus is in your heart, you can ask for the Holy Spirit to come in, and He will completely transform your life for not just the better but for the glory of God!

God can do anything, you know- far more than you could ever imagine or guess or request in your wildest dreams! He does it not by pushing us around but by working within us, his Spirit deeply and gently within us. Glory to God in the church! Glory to God in the Messiah, in Jesus! Glory down all the generations! Glory through the millennia! Oh yes! Ephesians 3:20 MSG

Salvation Prayer:

Jesus, I need You. I am a sinner, but today, I repent of all my sins! I believe with all my heart and confess with my mouth that You died on the cross for me. You were buried, and on the third day, You rose again. I repent of all my sins and ask and receive Your forgiveness. Wash me in your blood. Come into my heart and make me new. Heal all the brokenness in me, and let Your glory shine through. I am now Yours, and You are now mine. I make You my Lord, Savior, and King over my entire life. In Jesus' name, I receive salvation made available only by You, Jesus. Amen.

And that message is the very message about faith that we preach: If you openly declare that Jesus is Lord and believe in your heart that God raised him from the dead, you will be saved. Romans 10:8-9

"For it is by believing in your heart that you are made right with God, and it is by openly declaring your faith that you are saved." Romans 10:10

For "Everyone who calls on the name of the LORD will be saved." Romans 10:13

Baptism of the Holy Spirit Prayer:

Jesus, You said in Your word that when we receive and make You our personal Lord and Savior, You would give us a gift. You came to baptize us in water, which I will do upon making You my Savior, but also in fire. The Holy Spirit is this fire, and I ask for the baptism of the Holy Spirit with evidence from tongues. Baptize me and fill me with the Holy Spirit in Jesus' name, I ask, Amen.

As an act of faith, I open my mouth, and I am going to speak in tongues. Tip: Just begin to open your mouth and make some sound you feel deep inside, and the Holy Spirit will come out. You look normal in Heaven doing this, by the way! I encourage you to pray daily for a part of your day, and you can do this anywhere all the time! Be consistent, and you'll get consistent results, maybe even more! Have fun!

Peter replied, "Each of you must repent of your sins and turn to God, and be baptized in the name of Jesus Christ for the forgiveness of your sins. Then you will receive the gift of the Holy Spirit." Acts of the Apostles 2:38

"This promise is to you, to your children, and to those far away- all who have been called by the Lord our God." Acts of the Apostles 2:39

"But in fact, it is best for you that I go away, because if I don't, the Advocate won't come. If I do go away, then I will send him to you." John 16:7

"But I will send you the Advocate- the Spirit of truth. He will come to you from the Father and will testify all about me. John 15:26

'In the last days,' God says, 'I will pour out my Spirit upon all people. Your sons and daughters will prophesy. Your young men will see visions, and your old men will dream dreams. In those days I will pour out my Spirit even on my servants- men and women alike- and they will prophesy.' Acts of the Apostles 2:17-18

"Let love be your highest goal! But you should also desire the special abilities the Spirit gives— especially the ability to prophesy" 1 Corinthians 14:1

Bibliography

Definition of Self-Esteem by Oxford Dictionary on Lexico.com Also Meaning of Self-Esteem." Lexico Dictionaries | English, Lexico Dictionaries, www.lexico.com/definition/self-esteem.

Merriam–Webster Thesaurus, Abide is…: "Abide (v)," accessed December 15, 2020, Abide Synonyms, Abide Antonyms | Merriam-Webster Thesaurus (merriam-webster.com)

Merriam–Webster Dictionary, Trust is…: "Trust (n)," accessed December 30, 2020, Trust | Definition of Trust by Merriam-Webster (merriam-webster.com)

Orr, James, M.A., D.D. General Editor. "Entry for 'SARAH; SARAI.'" "International Standard Bible Encyclopedia". 1915. Sarah; Sarai Definition and Meaning - Bible Dictionary (biblestudytools.com) accessed December 28, 2020.

Jackson, Wayne. "The Allegory of the Vine and the Branches." Christian Courier, christiancourier.com/articles/the-allegory-of-the-vine-and-the-branches. Accessed 13 Mar. 2025. Original article from December 30, 2020 updated to one accessed

March 13,2025

Hey Y'all, my name is Savanna Watson. Thank you for picking up this book. I am a born again Believer in Jesus Christ and also a Texan, so I am doubly blessed! I have enjoyed writing throughout my life, but never imagined I would write a book, let alone books. I never knew how much writing would be a part of the destiny God has for me. I give all glory to God, Jesus and the Holy Spirit for allowing me to steward the revelations of the heart of God. I pray you encounter God's heart in each chapter and step into the story He has for you!